A DESCRIPTIVE GUIDE TO

COINS &

Edited by
Tom Michael &
George S. Cuhaj

CURRENCY

OF THE MIDDLE EAST

©2006 KP Books
Published by

kp books
An Imprint of F+W Publications

700 East State Street • Iola, WI 54990-0001
715-445-2214 • 888-457-2873

Our toll-free number to place an order or obtain
a free catalog is (800) 258-0929.

Library of Congress Catalog Number: 2005924833

ISBN: 0-89689-229-8

Designed by Kara Grundman
Edited by Tom Michael and George S. Cuhaj

Printed in the United States of America

CONTENTS

INTRODUCTION

Welcome to our presentation of Coins & Currency of the Middle East! In these pages you will find coverage of modern coins and banknotes dating from the Iranian Hostage Crisis to the current War in Iraq, along with various items of related ephemera from this region and time frame. We have tried to keep the book focused and concise to allow the reader to quickly locate an item in the text or images and in short order, learn a bit about what they have.

Some of you may have brought back keepsakes from your overseas service in Middle East nations. Others may have retained pocket change or trinkets from vacation and business travel to the region. Many of you may simply have friends, relatives, sons and daughters, serving overseas and have developed a curiosity for the objects of daily life, which seem so foreign to those of our own country.

Whatever may bring you to this book we hope that it's full color illustrations, concise descriptions, lively format and broad scope will satisfy your needs.

For simplicities sake we have grouped our chapters into major sections. The first section covers items of commerce. Here you will find listings and pictures of Coins, Paper Money, and Military tokens, commonly known as Pogs. The second section deals with service related items, centering on Military Medals and Challenge Coins. Also presented in this section is a brief listing of Commemorative Medals and tokens linked to the Middle East region. The third section covers paper items, with chapters on Books, Comic Books and Propaganda leaflets. Finally we have included a Memorabilia section which offers a wide array of items brought home by tourists and military personnel,

as well as items found back in the good old U.S.A. which pertain to our involvement in the Middle East over the past 25 years or so.

Once you've had a chance to peruse the body of the book, you may find yourself wanting to expand your scope of interest in this field. To assist the reader in this task we offer several appendices aimed at furthering your knowledge in the Middle East areas of geography, conflict history, numeral systems and dating systems. We have also complied a brief list of web sites, which may prove useful for additional study, identification and value assessment of Middle East items

In the case of coins and bank notes, you may also want to reference one of our larger Standard Catalogs for additional detailed information. We offer a full line of Standard Catalogs covering all aspects of coins and banknotes from 1600 to present.

If you are thinking of expanding your accumulation into a collection, or are considering disposing of unwanted items you may now posses, we highly recommend you get familiar with the Ebay Auction web site. There you will find many Middle East items being sold every day in all of the categories and topical areas encompassed in the chapters of this book.

Whatever your direction, we hope this book proves to be entertaining, enlightening and above all, useful for your needs.

Best,
Tom Michael and George Cuhaj

CONTRIBUTOR LISTING

A special "Thanks" is extended to the following individuals who offered their assistance most graciously during the creation of this volume.

John Adams-Graf	Armen Hovsepian	Mark Rhea
Colin R. Bruce II	Chet Krause	Ellen Robinson
Jimmy Cady	Frank McCarville	Shelley Robinson
Kenneth Douglas	Mary McCarville	Don Smith
Brent Frankenhoff	Kevin Michalowski	Daniel Springer
Herbert Fiedman	John Jackson Miller	Shelley Stockard
Steve Firebaugh	N. Douglas Nicol	Addison Tower
Raul Gonzalez	Sue Vater Olsen	Bobby Wierzba
Ross Hansen	Joseph Petrosius	Jennie Wierzba
		Chris Williams

COMMERCE

COINS

The coins of many Middle East nations have a character all their own. The differences in language and calendar are immediately evident and set these coins apart from what most American's are used to handling. These differences can provide an air of mystery and a distinct challenge for the military personnel serving in the Middle East. These comparative differences are often all that is needed to start a person along the path to coin collecting.

We hope this book will be both entertaining for the reader and helpful for the beginning collector of coins from this region. We have made every effort to offer a wide array of large color photographs along with succinct descriptions and a range of values, to give the reader an opportunity to identify coins they may have brought home and get some idea of their nature and value.

The coins in this section are first organized by country, then by series or date and finally by denomination or face value. Dates are given as they are read on the coin. If the coin is dual dated, both dates are given. If there are several dates in use for a particular type of coin, a date range will be given with first and last known dates separated by a dash.

Coin descriptions have been kept purposefully brief for ease of use. A description of the obverse or front of the coin is presented first, a description of the reverse or back follows. The two are simply separated by a slash mark.

Denominations or face values are presented as they read on the coin. To assist the reader in translating dates and denominations we have included a numeral chart in the appendix.

Values are presented for **worn** or circulated and **new** or uncirculated states of preservation. The term circulated, means that a coin has been used in commerce. It will have wear resulting from this normal use and handling.

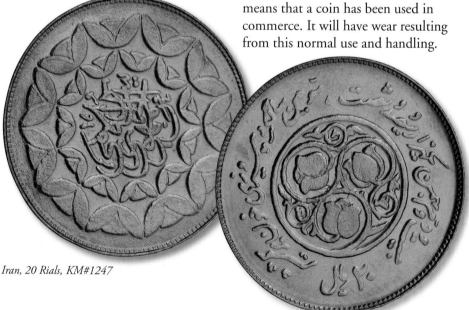

Iran, 20 Rials, KM#1247

The term uncirculated refers to a coin, which has never been used in trade. Uncirculated coins show no wear what so ever and appear to be brand new, just as when they were issued.

Finally we would like to offer a bit of advice regarding care, and preservation as well as buying and selling of coins. First of all, do not clean your coins, as you will most likely do more damage to them than good. Second, the best storage containers for most coins are made of non-acid paper, or of inert plastic such as Mylar. Soft plastic holders, leather pouches or manila envelopes will harm your coins if used for long-term storage. Your local coin dealer, a coin show, a coin newspaper or the Internet are all good sources for acquiring proper storage supplies for your coins. The same places are also where you would want to go to buy more coins or to sell the coins you currently own. In the general introduction to this book you will find additional advice regards these topics.

Afghanistan

	Worn	New
25 Pul, SH1357 (1978), KM#990, Aluminum-Bronze, Arms with writing/Denomination	$0.50	$2.00

	Worn	New
50 Pul, SH1357 (1978), KM#992, Aluminum-Bronze, Arms with writing/Denomination	$0.80	$2.50

	Worn	New
Afghani, SH1357 (1978), KM#993, Copper-Nickel, Arms with writing/Denomination	$1.00	$4.00
2 Afghanis, SH1357 (1978), KM#994, Copper-Nickel, Arms with writing/Denomination	$1.50	$4.00
5 Afghanis, SH1357 (1978), KM#995, Copper-Nickel, Arms with writing/Denomination	$2.00	$6.50

	Worn	New
25 Pul, SH1359 (1980), KM#996, Aluminum-Bronze, Arms with rising sun/ Denomination	$0.35	$1.50
50 Pul, SH1359 (1980), KM#997, Aluminum-Bronze, Arms with rising sun/ Denomination	$0.50	$2.00
Afghani, SH1359 (1980), KM#998, Copper-Nickel, Arms with rising sun/ Denomination	$0.80	$2.50
2 Afghanis, SH1359 (1980), KM#999, Copper-Nickel, Arms with rising sun/ Denomination	$1.00	$3.00
5 Afghanis, SH1359 (1980), KM#1000, Copper-Nickel, Arms with rising sun/ Denomination	$1.50	$4.00

	Worn	New
5 afghanis, SH1360 (1981), KM#1001, Brass, Arms with rising sun/ FAO and grain	$0.50	$1.75
10 Afghanis, 1989, KM#1015, Brass, Archway/ Legends	$1.00	$3.50

Djibouti

	Worn	New
Franc, 1977-1996, KM#20, Aluminum, Arms/Antelope	$0.75	$3.00

	Worn	New
2 Francs, 1977, KM#21, Aluminum, Arms/Antelope	$1.00	$3.50

Afghanistan, 5 Afghanis, SH1357 (1978), KM#995

	Worn	New
5 Francs, 1977-1991, KM#22, Aluminum, Arms/ Antelope	$1.25	$4.00

10 Francs, 1977-1996, KM#23, Aluminum-Bronze, Arms/Boats $0.75 $2.50

	Worn	New
20 Francs, 1977-1996, KM#24, Aluminum-Bronze, Arms/Boats	$0.75	$2.50
50 Francs, 1977-1991, KM#25, Copper-Nickel, Arms/Camels	$1.50	$5.50

100 Francs, 1977-1991, KM#26, Copper-Nickel, Arms/Camels $2.00 $6.50

500 Francs, 1989-1991, KM#27, Aluminum-Bronze, Arms/Denomination $4.00 $10.00

10 Francs, 2003, KM#34, Copper-Nickel, Arms/Chimpanzee $0.50 $1.00

Djibouti 50 Francs, 1977-1991, KM#25

	Worn	New
Millieme, AH1392-AD1972, KM#A423, Aluminum, Date and denomination/Arms	$0.10	$0.50
5 Milliemes, AH1392-AD1972, KM#A424, Aluminum, Date and denomination/FAO	$10.00	$45.00
5 Milliemes, AH1392-AD1972, KM#A425, Aluminum, Date and denomination/Arms, 21mm	$0.20	$2.50
5 Milliemes, AH1393-AD1973, KM#432, Brass, Date and denomination/Arms, 17.5mm	$0.10	$0.30
5 Milliemes, AH1393-AD1973, KM#433, Aluminum, Date and denomination/Arms, 21mm	$10.00	$45.00
10 Milliemes, AH1392-AD1972, KM#A426, Aluminum, Date and denomination/Arms	$0.50	$6.00
10 Milliemes, AH1393-AD1973, KM#435, Brass, Date and denomination/Arms	$0.10	$0.50
10 Milliemes, AH1396-AD1976, KM#435, Brass, Date and denomination/Arms	$0.75	$3.00

	Worn	New
2 Piastres, AH1404-AD1984, KM#554.2, Aluminum-Bronze, Islamic date left of denomination	$0.10	$0.50
5 Piastres, AH1392-AD1972, KM#A428, Copper-Nickel, Date and denomination/Arms	$0.50	$2.00
5 Piastres, AH1396-AD1976, KM#450, Copper-Nickel, Date and denomination/Arms	$5.00	$20.00

Piastre, AH1404-AD1984, KM#553.1, Aluminum-Bronze, Christian date left of denomination — $0.10 / $0.35

Piastre, AH1404-AD1984, KM#553.2, Aluminum-Bronze, Islamic date left of denomination — $0.10 / $0.35

2 Piastres, AH1404-AD1984, KM#554.1, Aluminum-Bronze, Christian date left of denomination — $0.10 / $0.50

Egyptian, 5 Piastres, AH1404-AD1984, KM#555.2

	Worn	New
5 Piastres, AH1404-AD1984, KM#555.1, Aluminum-Bronze, Christian date left of denomination	$0.20	$0.75
5 Piastres, AH1404-AD1984, KM#555.2, Aluminum-Bronze, Islamic date left of denomination	$0.20	$0.75
5 Piastres, AH1404-AD1984, KM#622.1, Aluminum-Bronze, Christian date left of denomination	$0.20	$0.85
5 Piastres, AH1404-AD1984, KM#622.2, Aluminum-Bronze, Islamic date left of denomination	$0.20	$0.85

	Worn	New
10 Piastres, AH1404-AD1984, KM#556, Copper-Nickel, Date and denomination/Mosque	$0.25	$0.85

	Worn	New
10 Piastres, AH1413-AD1992, KM#732, Brass, Date and denomination/Mosque	$0.20	$1.25
20 Piastres, AH1400-AD1980, KM#507, Copper-Nickel, Date and denomination/Arms	$0.75	$2.35

	Worn	New
5 Piastres, AH1413-AD1992, KM#731, Brass, Date and denomination/Vase	$0.20	$0.85
10 Piastres, AH1392-AD1972, KM#430, Copper-Nickel, Date and denomination/Arms	$0.60	$2.50
10 Piastres, AH1396-AD1976, KM#431, Copper-Nickel, Date and denomination/Arms	$5.50	$27.50

Egyptian, 20 Piastres, AH1400-AD1980

	Worn	New
20 Piastres, AH1425-AD2004, KM#923, Copper-Nickel, Denomination and date/Woman and Sphinx	$1.25	$2.50

	Worn	New
20 Piastres, AH1404-AD1984, KM#557, Copper-Nickel, Date and denomination/Mosque	$0.45	$1.65
20 Piastres, AH1413-AD1992, KM#733, Copper-Nickel, Date and denomination/Mosque	$0.60	$2.50

	Worn	New
5 Milliemes, AH1393-AD1973, KM#433, Aluminum, Date and denomination/FAO	$0.10	$0.35

	Worn	New
5 Milliemes, AH1397-AD1977, KM#462, Brass, Date and denomination/Cattle and farmers	$0.10	$0.50
10 Milliemes, AH1395-AD1975, KM#446, Brass, Date and denomination/Agricultural workers	$0.10	$0.35
10 Milliemes, AH1396-AD1976, KM#449, Brass, Denomination and Date/Osiris and wheat	$0.10	$0.30
10 Milliemes, AH1397-AD1977, KM#464, Brass, Date and denomiantion/Figures in circle	$0.10	$0.85

	Worn	New
25 Piastres, AH1413-AD1993, KM#734, Copper-Nickel, Date/Denomination, holed as struck	$0.75	$2.75
5 Milliemes, AH1393-AD1973, KM#434, Brass, Date and denomination/Nefertiti	$5.00	$20.00
5 Milliemes, AH1395-AD1975, KM#445, Brass, Date and denomination/Nefertiti	$0.10	$0.30
5 Piastres, AH1395-AD1975, KM#447, Copper-Nickel, Date and denomination.Nefertiti	$0.50	$1.25
10 Piastres, AH1425-AD2004, KM#922, Copper-Nickel, Denomination and date/Woman and Sphinx	$0.75	$1.50

Egyptian, 2 Piastres, AH1400-AD1980, KM#500

PHOTO BY STAFF SGT. CHARLES B. JOHNSON

	Worn	New
10 Milliemes, AH1398-AD1978, KM#476, Brass, Date and denomiantion/Woman with microscope, FAO	$0.10	$0.80

10 Milliemes, AH1400-AD1980, KM#499, Aluminum-Bronze, Date and denomination / Woman Kneeling, FAO	$0.10	$0.60
2 Piastres, AH1400-AD1980, KM#500, Aluminum-Bronze, Date and denomination/FAO	$0.20	$0.60
5 Piastres, AH1397-AD1977, KM#468, Copper-Nickel, Date and denomination/FAO	$0.50	$1.65

5 Piastres, AH1398-AD1978, KM#478, Copper-Nickel, Date and denomination/FAO	$0.50	$1.65
10 Piastres, AH1395-AD1975, KM#448, Copper-Nickel, Date and denomination/FAO	$0.60	$3.50
10 Piastres, AH1397-AD1977, KM#469, Copper-Nickel, Date and denomination/FAO	$0.60	$2.25

10 Piastres, AH1400-AD1980, KM#505, Copper-Nickel, Date and denomination/ Woman Kneeling, FAO	$0.50	$2.25

5 Milliemes, AH1397-AD1977, KM#463, Brass, Date and denomination/Bust left, sun above	$0.10	$0.50

	Worn	New
5 Milliemes, AH1399-AD1979, KM#463, Brass, Date and denomination/Bust left, sun above	$0.10	$0.50
10 Milliemes, AH1397-AD1977, KM#465, Brass, Date and denomination/Bust left, sun above	$0.10	$0.65

10 milliemes, AH1399-AD1979, KM#465, Brass, Date and denomination/Bust left, sun above	$0.20	$1.00
5 Piastres, AH1397-AD1977, KM#466, Copper-Nickel, Date and denomination/Bust left, sun above	$0.50	$1.50
5 Piastres, AH1399-AD1979, KM#466, Copper-Nickel, Date and denomination/Bust left, sun above	$0.50	$1.25
10 Piastres, AH1397-AD1977, KM#470, Copper-Nickel, Date and denomination/Bust left, sun above	$0.50	$2.50
10 Piastres, AH1399-AD1979, KM#470, Copper-Nickel, Date and denomination/Bust left, sun above	$0.50	$2.50

PHOTO BY: SPC. MICHAEL J. CARDEN, 3RD BRIGADE COMBAT TEAM PUBLIC AFFAIRS, 82ND AIRBORNE DIVISION

Egyptian, 5 Milliemes, AH1399-AD1979, KM#463

	Worn	New
10 Milliemes, AH1399-AD1979, KM#483, Brass, Date and denomination/Seated mother with child	$0.10	$0.65

5 Piastres, AH1399-AD1979, KM#484,
Copper-Nickel, Date and denomination/Seated
mother with child — $0.50 — $1.65

10 Milliemes, AH1400-AD1980, KM#498,
Aluminum-Bronze, Raised fist/Denomination
and date — $0.10 — $1.00

Egyptian, 5 Piastres,
AH1397-AD1977,
KM#466

	Worn	New
5 Piastres, AH1400-AD1980, KM#502, Copper-Nickel, Raised fist/Denomination and date	$0.50	$1.75

	Worn	New
10 Piastres, AH1400-AD1980, KM#506, Copper-Nickel, Raised fist/Denomination and date	$0.50	$2.25
10 Piastres, AH1401-AD1981, KM#506, Copper-Nickel, Raised fist/Denomination and date	$0.60	$3.50
5 Piastres, AH1392-AD1972, KM#A427, Copper-Nickel	$0.75	$3.00
5 Piastres, AH1393-AD1973, KM#436, Copper-Nickel	$0.60	$2.25
5 Piastres, AH1393-AD1973, KM#437, Copper-Nickel, Date and denomination/Globe and Bank building	$0.60	$2.00
25 Piastres, AH1393-AD1973, KM#438, Silver, Date and denomination/Globe and Bank building	$4.00	$9.00
5 Piastres, AH1394-AD1974, KM#A441, Copper- Nickel, Date and denomination/Soldier with gun	$0.60	$2.00
10 Piastres, AH1394-AD1974, KM#442, Copper- Nickel, Date and denomination/Soldier with gun	$0.60	$3.50

10 Piastres, AH1410-AD1989, KM#675,Copper-
Nickel, Date, denomination and Toughra/Raised Flag
and building — $0.75 — $1.75

	Worn	New
20 Piastres, AH1410-AD1989, KM#676, Copper-Nickel, Date, denomination and Toughra/ Raised Flag and building	$1.00	$2.50
5 Piastres, AH1396-AD1976, KM#451, Copper-Nickel, Cairo Trade fair	$0.60	$2.00
5 Piastres, AH1397-AD1977, KM#467, Copper-Nickel, Textile industry	$0.50	$1.65

	Worn	**New**
5 Piastres, AH1398-AD1978, KM#477, Copper-Nickel, Date and denomination/Industrial view	**$0.50**	**$1.65**

	Worn	**New**
10 Piastres, AH1399-AD1979, KM#485, Copper-Nickel, Denomination and date/Mint building	**$0.50**	**$2.25**

	Worn	New
5 Piastres, AH1400-AD1980, KM#501, Copper-Nickel, Date and denomination/Professionals at work	$0.50	$1.35
10 Piastres, AH1392-AD1972, KM#429, Copper-Nickel	$0.60	$2.50
10 Piastres, AH1398-AD1978, KM#479, Copper-Nickel	$0.50	$2.75
10 Piastres, AH1396-AD1976, KM#452, Copper-Nickel, Suez Canal	$0.60	$3.50
10 Piastres, AH1397-AD1977, KM#471, Copper-Nickel	$0.50	$2.25

	Worn	New
10 Piastres, AH1399-AD1979, KM#486, Copper-Nickel, Date and denomination/Classrooms	$0.50	$2.25

Egyptian, 10 Piastres,
AH1401-AD1981,
KM#506

	Worn	New
10 Piastres, AH1400-AD1980, KM#503,
Copper-Nickel, Denomination and date/Seated
Egyptian healer with staff — $0.50 — $2.50

	Worn	New
10 Piastres, AH1401-AD1981, KM#520,
Copper-Nickel, Denomination and date/Rising sun
over Satellite dish — $0.50 — $2.25

10 Piastres, AH1400-AD1980, KM#504,
Copper-Nickel, Denomination and date/Anwar Sadat,
Dove and signed Treaty — $1.00 — $3.50

10 Piastres, AH1402-AD1981, KM#521,
Copper-Nickel, Date and denomination/Shield — $1.00 — $3.50

Sergeant Bill Whittaker, of 361st Psychological Operations Battalion, shakes hands with an Iraqi boy during a patrol in Mosul, Iraq on December 13, 2004. SGT Whittaker is handing out fliers while on a foot patrol with Charlie Company, 1st Battalion, 24th Infantry Regiment, 1st Brigade 25th Infantry Division Stryker Brigade Combat Team (SBCT). 1/25 SBCT is in Iraq in support of Operation Iraqi Freedom.

U.S. ARMY PHOTOS BY SGT. JEREMIAH JOHNSON

	Worn	**New**

10 Piastres, AH1402-AD1982, KM#599,
Copper-Nickel, Date and denomination/
Company symbol — **$0.50** **$2.25**

10 Piastres, AH1405-AD1985, KM#570, Copper-
Nickel, Legend and date/Shield with legend below — **$0.35** **$1.75**

10 Pistares, AH1405-AD1985, KM#573, Copper-Nickel,
Legend and date/Parliament building — **$0.35** **$1.75**

20 Piastres, AH1405-AD1985, KM#596,
Copper-Nickel, Legend and date/Birds making
diamond shape — **$0.75** **$2.25**

20 Piastres, AH1405-AD1985, KM#597,
Copper-Nickel, Legend and date/
Professionals at work — **$0.75** **$2.50**

20 Piastres, AH1406-AD1986, KM#606,
Copper-Nickel, Legend and date/Crossed swords — **$0.75** **$2.50**

	Worn	**New**

20 Piastres, AH1407-AD1986, KM#607,
Copper-Nickel, Legend and date/City scene — **$0.75** **$2.25**

20 Piastres, AH1407-AD1987, KM#652,
Copper-Nickel, Toughra and date/English legend,
symbol in circle — **$0.75** **$2.50**

20 Piastres, AH1408-AD1988, KM#646,
Copper-Nickel, Legend and date/Bird in wreath — **$1.00** **$2.75**

20 Piastres, AH1409-AD1988, KM#650,
Copper-Nickel, Legend and date/Opera House
building — **$0.75** **$2.50**

20 Piastres, AH1409-AD1989, KM#685,
Copper-Nickel, Date and denomination in circle/
Map, crescent and figures — **$0.75** **$2.50**

20 Piastres, AH1409-AD1989, KM#690,
Copper-Nickel, Four cubes/Subway train — **$1.00** **$2.75**

20 Piastres,
AH1409-AD1989,
KM#690

	Worn	New
Cent, EE1969 (1977), KM#43.1, Aluminum, Small lion head, uniform chin whiskers/Farmer with Oxen	$0.30	$1.00
Cent, EE1969 (1977), KM#43.2, Aluminum, Small lion head, two long chin whiskers/Farmer with Oxen	$0.35	$1.25
Cent, EE1969 (1977), KM#43.3, Aluminum, Large lion head/Farmer with Oxen - Franklin Mint Proof		$2.50
5 Cents, EE1969 (1977), KM#44.1, Copper-Zinc, Small lion head, uniform chin whiskers/Figure walking	$0.30	$1.00
5 Cents, EE1969 (1977), KM#44.2, Copper-Zinc, Small lion head, two long chin whiskers/ Figure walking	$0.35	$1.25
5 Cents, EE1969 (1977), KM#44.3, Copper-Zinc, Large lion head/Figure walking - Franklin Mint Proof		$2.50
10 Cents, EE1969 (1977), KM#45.1, Copper-Zinc, Small lion head, uniform chin whiskers/ Mountain Nyala	$0.30	$1.50
10 Cents, EE1969 (1977), KM#45.2, Copper-Zinc, Small lion head, two long chin whiskers/ Mountain Nyala	$0.40	$1.75
10 Cents, EE1969 (1977), KM#45.3, Copper-Zinc, Large lion head/Mountain Nyala - Franklin Mint Proof		$4.00

	Worn	New
25 Cents, EE1969 (1977), KM#46.1, Copper-Nickel, Small lion head, uniform chin whiskers/Couple with arms raised	$0.30	$1.25
25 Cents, EE1969 (1977), KM#46.2, Copper-Nickel, Small lion head, two long chin whiskers/Couple with arms raised	$0.40	$1.50
25 Cents, EE1969 (1977), KM#46.3, Copper-Nickel, Large lion head/Couple with arms raised - Franklin Mint Proof		$4.50
50 Cents, EE1969 (1977), KM#47.1, Copper-Nickel, Small lion head, uniform chin whiskers/Five figures	$0.75	$3.00
50 Cents, EE1969 (1977), KM#47.2, Copper-Nickel, Small lion head, two long chin whiskers/Five figures	$0.85	$3.00
50 Cents, EE1969 (1977), KM#47.3, Copper-Nickel, Large lion head/Five figures - Franklin Mint Proof		$7.50
2 Birr, EE1964 (1972)(error), KM#64, Copper-Nickel, Lion head/World Soccer Games 1982		$145.00
2 Birr, EE1974 (1982), KM#64, Copper-Nickel, Lion head/World Soccer Games 1982		$10.00

2 Birr, EE1964 (1972)(error), KM#64

	Worn	New
Rial, SH1357 (1978), KM#1172, Copper-Nickel, Date, denomination, crown above/Lion with sword	$2.00	$7.00
2 Rials, MS2536 (1977), KM#1174, Copper-Nickel, Date, denomination, crown above/Lion with sword	$0.50	$4.00
2 Rials, MS2537 (1978), KM#1174, Copper-Nickel, Date, denomination, crown above/Lion with sword	$0.50	$4.00
2 Rials, SH1357 (1978), KM#1174, Copper-Nickel, Date, denomination, crown above/Lion with sword	$2.50	$10.00
5 Rials, MS2536 (1977), KM#1176, Copper-Nickel, Date, denomination, crown above/ Lion with sword	$0.50	$3.50
5 Rials, MS2537 (1978), KM#1176, Copper-Nickel, Date, denomination, crown above/Lion with sword	$0.65	$3.50

	Worn	New
50 Dinars, SH1357 (1978), KM#1156a, Brass-Coated Steel Lion with sword/ denomination in wreath	$5.00	$15.00
50 Dinars, SH1358 (1979), KM#1156a, Brass-Coated Steel Lion with sword/ denomination in wreath	$8.00	$25.00
Rial, MS2536 (1977), KM#1172, Copper-Nickel, Date, denomination, crown above/Lion with sword	$2.00	$7.00
Rial, MS2537 (1978), KM#1172, Copper-Nickel, Date, denomination, crown above/Lion with sword	$2.00	$7.00

	Worn	New
Rial, SH1357/6 (1978), KM#1172, Copper-Nickel, Date, denomination, crown above/Lion with sword	$0.50	$5.00
5 Rials, SH1357 (1978), KM#1176, Copper-Nickel, Date, denomination, crown above/Lion with sword	$2.50	$10.00

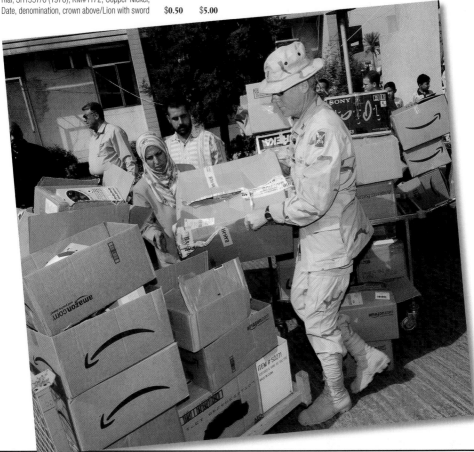

	Worn	New
10 Rials, MS2536 (1977), KM#1179, Copper-Nickel, Bust left/Crown above lion with sword	$0.60	$3.00

	Worn	New
10 Rials, MS2537 (1978), KM#1179, Copper-Nickel, Bust left/Crown above lion with sword	$0.60	$4.00
10 Rials, SH1357 (1978), KM#1179, Copper-Nickel, Bust left/Crown above lion with sword	$5.00	$15.00
20 Rials, MS2536 (1977), KM#1181, Copper-Nickel, Bust left/Crown above lion with sword	$0.75	$4.00
20 Rials, MS2537 (1978), KM#1181, Copper-Nickel, Bust left/Crown above lion with sword	$0.75	$4.00

	Worn	New
20 Rials, SH1357 (1978), KM#1214, Copper-Nickel, Bust left/Bust left	$5.00	$13.50

	Worn	New
20 Rials, SH1357 (1978), KM#1181, Copper-Nickel, Bust left/Crown above lion with sword	$1.00	$5.00
20 Rials, SH1357 (1978), KM#1215, Copper-Nickel, Bust left/Lion with sword, crown above, FAO below	$0.75	$6.00
1/4 Pahlavi, MS2536 (1977), KM#1198, Gold, Bust left/Crown above lion with sword, 16mm	$26.00	$35.00
1/4 Pahlavi, MS2537 (1978), KM#1198, Gold, Bust left/Crown above lion with sword, 16mm	$26.00	$35.00
1/4 Pahlavi, SH1358 (1979), KM#1198, Gold, Bust left/Crown above lion with sword, 16mm	$250.00	$400.00
1/2 Pahlavi, MS2536 (1977), KM#1199, Gold, Bust left/Crown above lion with sword, 18mm	$55.00	$65.00
1/2 Pahlavi, MS2537 (1978), KM#1199, Gold, Bust left/Crown above lion with sword, 18mm	$55.00	$65.00
1/2 Pahlavi, SH1358 (1979), KM#1199, Gold, Bust left/Crown above lion with sword, 18mm	$250.00	$750.00
Pahlavi, MS2536 (1977), KM#1200, Gold, Bust left/Crown above lion with sword, 21.5mm	$105.00	$125.00
Pahlavi, MS2537 (1978), KM#1200, Gold, Bust left/Crown above lion with sword, 21.5mm	$105.00	$125.00
Pahlavi, SH1358 (1979), KM#1200, Gold, Bust left/Crown above lion with sword, 21.5mm	$250.00	$750.00
2 1/2 Pahlavi, MS2536 (1977), KM#1201, Gold, Bust left/Crown above lion with sword, 28.5mm	$255.00	$285.00
2 1/2 Pahlavi, MS2537 (1978), KM#1201, Gold, Bust left/Crown above lion with sword, 28.5mm	$255.00	$285.00
2 1/2 Pahlavi, MS2538 (1979), KM#1201, Gold, Bust left/Crown above lion with sword, 28.5mm	$300.00	$750.00

U.S. ARMY PHOTO BY SPC. SEAN KIMMONS

2 1/2 Pahlavi, SH1358 (1979), KM#1201, Gold,
Bust left/Crown above lion with sword, 28.5mm $300.00 $750.00

5 Pahlavi, MS2536 (1977), KM#1202, Gold, Bust
left/Crown above lion with sword, 39mm $510.00 $540.00

5 Pahlavi, MS2537 (1978), KM#1202, Gold, Bust
left/Crown above lion with sword, 39mm $510.00 $540.00

5 Pahlavi, SH1358 (1979), KM#1202, Gold, Bust
left/Crown above lion with sword, 39mm $1,250.00 $1,750.00

10 Pahlavi, MS2536 (1977), KM#1212, Gold,
Conjoined busts left/Legen with crown above,
48.5mm $1,000.00 $1,150.00

10 Pahlavi, MS2537 (1978), KM#1213, Gold, Bust
left/Crown above lion with sword, 48.5mm $1,000.00 $1,150.00

10 Pahlavi, SH1358 (1979), KM#1213, Gold, Bust
left/Crown above lion with sword, 48.5mm $3,250.00 $4,000.00

50 Dinars, SH1358 (1979), KM#1231, Brass Clad
Steel, Lion with sword/denomination in wreath $8.00 $25.00

Worn   New

Rial, SH1358-67 (1979-88), KM#1232,
Copper-Nickel, Legend/Denomination, 18mm $0.25 $1.75

2 Rials, SH1358-67 (1979-88), KM#1233,
Copper-Nickel, Legend/Denomination, 21mm $0.50 $3.25

5 Rials, SH1358-68 (1979-89), KM#1234,
Copper-Nickel, Legend/Denomination, 23.5mm $0.75 $3.50

*10 Rials, SH1358-61
(1979-82), KM#1235.1*

	Worn	New		Worn	New

10 Rials, SH1358-61 (1979-82), KM#1235.1, Copper-Nickel, Legend/ Denomination in wreath, 27mm — **$1.00** **$4.50**

10 Rials, SH1361-67 (1982-88), KM#1235.2, Copper-Nickel, Legend/ Denomination in revised wreath, 27mm — **$1.00** **$4.00**

20 Rials, SH1358-67 (1979-88), KM#1236, Copper-Nickel, Legend/ Denomination in wreath, 29mm — **$1.00** **$4.50**

50 Rials, SH1359-65 (1980-86), KM#1237.1, Aluminum-Bronze, Oil rigs, grain and denomination/ County map in relief — **$2.00** **$8.00**

50 Rials, SH1366-68 (1987-89), KM#1237.2, Aluminum-Bronze, Oil rigs, grain and denomination/ County map incuse — **$4.00** **$9.00**

50 Rials, SH1368-70 (1989-91), KM#1237.1a, Copper-Nickel, Oil rigs, grain and denomination/ County map in relief — **$2.00** **$7.50**

250 Rials, SH1372-82 (1993-2003), KM#1262, Copper-Nickel in Brass, Date and denomination in wreath/Stylized flower — **$4.50** **$7.50**

Rial, SH1359 (1980), KM#1245, Bronze Clad Steel, Denomination/Domed Mosque of Omar (World Jerusalem Day) — **$0.50** **$2.50**

10 Rials, SH1358 (1979), KM#1243, Copper-Nickel, Denomination in wreath/Flowers (1st Anniversary of Revolution) — **$1.50** **$4.50**

10 Rials, SH1368 (1989), KM#1253.1, Copper-Nickel, Dome, small denomination/Moslems Unite (World Jerusalem Day) — **$1.00** **$4.00**

10 Rials, SH1368 (1989), KM#1253.2, Copper-Nickel, Dome, large denomination/Moslems Unite (World Jerusalem Day) — **$1.00** **$4.00**

20 Rials, SH1358-AH1400 (1979), KM#1244, Copper-Nickel, Denomination in wreath/Globe and banner (1400th Anniversary of Mohammed's Flight) — **$2.50** **$5.00**

20 Rials, SH1359 (1980), KM#1246, Copper-Nickel, Denomination and flowers/Legend (2nd Anniversary of Islamic Revolution) — **$2.50** **$5.00**

20 Rials, SH1360 (1981), KM#1247, Copper-Nickel, Circle of flowers/Legend in double boarder (3rd Anniversary of Islamic Revolution) — **$2.50** **$5.00**

	Worn	New
20 Rials, SH1367 (1988), KM#1251, Copper-Nickel, Legend in wreath/Clasped hands over building (Islamic Banking Week)	$2.50	$5.00
20 Rials, SH1368 (1989), KM#1254.1, Copper-Nickel, Denomination 20 dots at rim/8 years of sacred defense within thin wreath	$2.50	$5.00

	Worn	New
20 Rials, SH1368 (1989), KM#1254.2, Copper-Nickel, Denomination 20 dots at rim/8 years of sacred defense within thick wreath	$2.50	$5.00
20 Rials, SH1368 (1989), KM#1254.3, Copper-Nickel, Denomination 22 dots at rim/8 years of sacred defense within wreath	$2.50	$5.00
50 Rials, SH1367 (1988), KM#1252, Copper-Nickel, Oil rigs, grain and denomination/Stylized flower (10th Anniversary of Islamic Revolution)	$3.00	$7.50
Rial, SH1371-74 (1992-95), KM#1263, Brass, Denomination and date/Mount Damavand	$5.00	$20.00

	Worn	New
5 Rials, SH1371-78 (1992-99), KM#1258, Brass, Denomination and date/Tomb of Hafez	$0.50	$3.00
10 Rials, SH1371-76 (1992-96), KM#1259, Aluminum-Bronze, Denomination and date/ Tomb of Ferdousi	$1.00	$3.75
50 Rials, SH1371-80 (1992-2001), KM#1260, Copper-Nickel, Denomination and date/Shrine of Hazrat Masumah	$2.50	$5.00

	Worn	New
100 Rials, SH1371-72 (1992-93), KM#1261.1, Copper-Nickel, Thin denomination and date/Shrine of Imam Reza	$4.00	$6.50

5 Rials, SH1371-78 (1992-99), KM#1258

Spc. Scott Brennan, a medic with the 725th Main Support Battalion, examines an Afghan boy's throat during a coopertive medical assistance mission Jan. 18 in Sadak, Afghanistan.

	Worn	New
100 Rials, SH1372-80 (1993-2001), KM#1261.2, Copper-Nickel, Thick denomination and date/Shrine of Imam Reza	$4.00	$6.50
50 Rials, SH1383 (2004), KM#1266, Aluminum-Bronze, Denomination in wreath, date below/Shrine of Hazrat Masumah	$3.00	$5.00
100 Rials, SH1383 (2004), KM#1267, Aluminum-Bronze, Denomination in wreath, date below/Shrine of Imam Reza	$4.00	$6.50
250 Rials, SH1383 (2004), KM#1268, Copper-Nickel, Denomination in wreath, date below/Stylized flower	$5.00	$7.50
500 Rials, SH1383 (2004), KM#1269, Aluminum-Bronze in Copper-Nickel, Denomination in circle, date below/Bird and flowers	$6.00	$8.50
1/4 Azadi, SH1358 (1979), KM#1238, Gold, Legend reads: 1st Spring of Freedom, Mosque, date below/Symbol, 15mm		$300.00
1/2 Azadi, SH1358 (1979), KM#1239, Gold, Legend reads: 1st Spring of Freedom, Mosque, date below/Symbol, 18mm		$100.00
Azadi, SH1358 (1979), KM#1240, Gold, Legend reads: 1st Spring of Freedom, Mosque, date below/Symbol, 21mm		$125.00
2 1/2 Azadi, SH1358 (1979), KM#1241, Gold, Legend reads: 1st Spring of Freedom, Mosque, date below/Symbol, 28mm		$1,500.00
5 Azadi, SH1358 (1979), KM#1242, Gold, Legend reads: 1st Spring of Freedom, Mosque, date below/Symbol, 40mm		$3,500.00

	Worn	New
1/4 Azadi, SH1366-70 (1987-91), KM#1265, Gold, Legend reads: Spring of Freedom, Mosque, date below/Symbol, 15mm		$300.00
1/2 Azadi, SH1363 (1984), KM#1250.1, Gold, Small legend reads: Spring of Freedom, Mosque, date below/Symbol, 18mm		$100.00
1/2 Azadi, SH1366-81 (1987-2002), KM#1250.2, Gold, Large legend reads: Spring of Freedom, Mosque, date below/Symbol, 18mm		$125.00
Azadi, SH1363 (1984), KM#1248.1, Gold, Small legend reads: Spring of Freedom, Mosque, date below/Symbol, 21mm		$120.00
Azadi, SH1364-70 (1985-91), KM#1248.2, Gold, Large legend reads: Spring of Freedom, Mosque, date below/Symbol, 21mm		$120.00
Azadi, SH1370 (1991), KM#A1264, Gold, Mosque/Bust of Khomeini left		$145.00
Azadi, SH1370-75 (1991-96), KM#1264, Gold, Mosque/Bust of Khomeini right		$125.00

Iraq

	Worn	New
5 Fils, 1971-1981, KM#125a, Stainless Steel, Legend and denomination/Palm Trees	$0.15	$0.35

	Worn	**New**
10 Fils, 1971-1981, KM#126a, Stainless Steel, Legend and denomination/Palm Trees	$0.30	$1.00

25 Fils, 1969-1981, KM#127, Copper-Nickel, Legend and denomination/Palm Trees	$0.30	$1.00

50 Fils, 1969-1990, KM#128, Copper-Nickel, Legend and denomination/Palm Trees	$0.35	$1.25

	Worn	**New**
100 Fils, 1970-1979, KM#129, Copper-Nickel, Legend and denomination/Palm Trees	$0.75	$3.00

250 Fils, 1980-1990, KM#147, Copper-Nickel, Legend and denomination/Palm Trees	$1.00	$5.00
500 Fils, 1982, KM#165, Nickel, Legend and denomination 500 Fals/ Palm Trees	$2.50	$7.00
500 Fils, 1982, KM#165a, Nickel, Legend and denomination 500 Falsan/ Palm Trees	$20.00	$85.00
Dinar, 1981, KM#170, Nickel, Legend and denomination/Palm Trees	$3.00	$6.50
5 Fils, 1982, KM#159, Stainless Steel, Legend and denomination/Babylon riuns	$0.15	$0.50

500 Fils, 1982, KM#165

	Worn	New
5 Fils, 1982, KM#159a, Copper-Nickel, Legend and denomination/Babylon riuns (proof)		$3.00
10 Fils, 1982, KM#160, Stainless Steel, Legend and denomination/Babylon, Ishtar Gate	$0.25	$0.75
10 Fils, 1982, KM#160a, Copper-Nickel, Legend and denomination/Babylon, Ishtar Gate (proof)		$3.00
50 Fils, 1982, KM#162, Copper-Nickel, Legend and denomination/Babylon Bull	$0.50	$2.50
50 Fils, 1982, KM#162, Copper-Nickel, Legend and denomination/Bull (proof)		$6.00
250 Fils, 1982, KM#163, Copper-Nickel, Legend and denomination/Babylon, Hammurabi Stele	$1.00	$4.50
250 Fils, 1982, KM#163, Copper-Nickel, Legend and denomination/Babylon, Hammurabi Stele (proof)		$8.00

250 Fils, 1979, KM#144

	Worn	New
500 Fils, 1982, KM#168, Nickel, Legend and denomination 500 Fals/Lion of Babylon	$2.00	$8.00
500 Fils, 1982, KM#168, Nickel, Legend and denomination 500 Fals/Lion of Babylon (proof)		$12.50

	Worn	New
500 Fils, 1982, KM#168a, Nickel, Legend and denomination 500 Falsan/Lion of Babylon	$15.00	$75.00
Dinar, 1982, KM#164, Nickel, Legend and denomination/Tower of Babylon	$3.50	$8.00
Dinar, 1982, KM#164, Nickel, Legend and denomination/Tower of Babylon (proof)		$12.50
5 Dinars, 1990, KM#171, Bronze, Denomination and legend/Two swords arched above palm tree (never officially released)		$5.00
10 Dinars, 1990, KM#172, Bronze, Denomination and legend/Two swords arched above palm tree (never officially released)		$10.00
250 Fils, 1979, KM#144, Nickel, Date and denomination/Bust of Child		$8.00

Worn New

Dinar, 1979, KM#145

Dinar, 1979, KM#145, Silver, Date and denomination/Bust of Child
$47.50

Dinar, 1980, KM#148, Silver, Legends and denominations/Hejira and Mosque (proof)
$50.00

250 Fils, 1980, KM#146, Copper-Nickel, Date and denomination/Bust of Saddam left
$3.00 $12.00

Dinar, 1980, KM#149, Nickel, Map above denomination/Bust of Saddam left
$7.00 $15.00

Chaplain (Capt.) Charles Seligman gives a local girl a bracelet during a humanitarian visit. The chaplain, along with volunteers from Balad Air Base, spent time at a local village handing out gifts as part of their mission to maintain and improve relations with Iraqis. He is assigned to the 332nd Air Expeditionary Wing.

Dinar, 1980, KM#149, Nickel Map above denomination/Bust of Saddam left (proof) — Worn: , New: $35.00

Dinar, 1981, KM#153, Nickel Denomination, date and legends/Bust of Saddam airplanes above — Worn: $10.00, New: $20.00

250 Fils, 1981, KM#152, Copper-Nickel, Legend, denomination and FAO/Date and view — Worn: $1.00, New: $4.00

Dinar, 1981, KM#153

	Worn	New
250 Fils, 1982, KM#155, Copper-Nickel, Legend and denomination/Date and Plam Tree	$1.00	$5.00

Dinar, 1982, KM#156, Nickel, Legend and denomination/Date and Palm Tree — Worn: $3.00, New: $8.00

25 Dinars, AH1425(2004), KM#175, Copper plated steel, Legend and denomination/Country map and date

	Worn	New
25 Dinars, AH1425(2004), KM#175, Copper plated steel, Legend and denomination/Country map and date		$2.50

100 Dinars, AH1425(2004), KM#176, Steel, Legend and denomination/Country map and date — $3.50

Israel

Agorah, JE5739-40 (1979-80), KM#24.1, Aluminum, Wheat/Denomination — $0.25 — $1.00

Agorah, JE5739 (1979), KM#24.2, Aluminum, Wheat, Star of David/Denomination — $1.00

	Worn	New
Agorah, JE5740 (1980), KM#96, Nickel, Wheat, Star of David/Denomination, 25th Anniversary Bank of Israel		$2.00
5 Agorot, JE5739 (1979), KM#25b, Aluminum, Pomegranates/Denomination		$0.50
5 Agorot, JE5739 (1979), KM#25c, Copper-Nickel, Pomagranates/Denomination, Star of David		$1.25
5 Agorot, JE5740 (1980), KM#97, Nickel, Pomagranates, Star of David/Denomination, 25th Anniversary Bank of Israel		$2.00
10 Agorot, JE5739-40 (1979-80), KM#26b, Aluminum, Palm tree, Star of David/Denomination		$0.25
10 Agorot, JE5739 (1979), KM#26c, Copper-Nickel, Palm tree, Star of David/Denomination		$1.00
10 Agorot, JE5740 (1980), KM#98, Nickel, Palm tree, Star of David/Denomination, 25th Anniversary Bank of Israel		$2.00

Agorah, JE5739-40 (1979-80), KM#24.1

The face of Sgt. Wesley Brown, missile shop NCOIC with Co. B 225th Forward Support Battalion, reflects off of an Improved Target Acquisition System while he cleans its viewfinder on Kirkuk Air Base Feb. 26. Brown is in charge of repairing the ITAS systems for the 2nd Brigade Combat Team, as they support Operation Iraqi Freedom II.

	Worn	New
25 Agorot, JE5739 (1979), KM#27, Aluminum - Bronze, Lyre/Denomination		$0.40
25 Agorot, JE5739 (1979), KM#27b, Copper-Nickel, Lyre, Star of David/Denomination		$1.50
25 Agorot, JE5740 (1980), KM#99, Nickel, Lyre, Star of David/Denomination, 25th Anniversary Bank of Israel		$2.00
1/2 Lirah, JE5739 (1979), KM#36.1, Copper-Nickel, Menorah/Denomination	$0.10	$0.50
1/2 Lirah, JE5739 (1979), KM#36.2, Copper-Nickel, Menorah, Star of David/Denomination		$1.00
1/2 Lirah, JE5740 (1980), KM#100, Nickel, Menorah, Star of David/Denomination, 25th Anniversary Bank of Israel		$3.00
Lirah, JE5740 (1980), KM#101, Nickel, Pomagranates, Menorah, Star of David/Denomination, 25th Anniversary Bank of Israel		$4.00
Lirah, JE5739-40 (1979-80), KM#47.1, Copper-Nickel, Pomagranates, Menorah/Denomination	$0.10	$0.75
Lirah, JE5739 (1979), KM#47.2, Copper-Nickel, Pomagranates, Menorah, Star of David/Denomination		$1.50
5 Lirot, JE5739 (1979), KM#90, Copper-Nickel, Lion, Menorah/Denomination	$0.35	$3.00
5 Lirot, JE5739 (1979), KM#90a, Copper-Nickel, Lion, Menorah, Star of David/Denomination		$3.50

	Worn	New
5 Lirot, JE5740 (1980), KM#102, Nickel, Lion, Menorah, Star of David/Denomination, 25th Anniversary Bank of Israel		$6.00

	Worn	New
New Agorah, JE5740-42 (1980-82), KM#106, Aluminum, Palm tree/Denomination		$0.20

	Worn	New
5 New Agorah, JE5740-42 (1980-82), KM#107, Aluminum, Menorah/Denomination		$0.20

1/2 Sheqel, JE5740-44 (1980-84), KM#109

	Worn	New
10 New Agorah, JE5740-44 (1980-84), KM#108, Bronze, Pomegranate/Denomination		$0.15
1/2 Sheqel, JE5740-44 (1980-84), KM#109, Copper-Nickel, Lion/Denomination		$0.65

	Worn	New
1/2 Sheqel, JE5743-AD1982, KM#121, Silver, Denomination/Holyland Sites, Qumran Caves		$10.00
1/2 Sheqel, JE5744-AD1983, KM#126, Silver, Denomination/Holyland Sites, Herodion Ruins		$10.00
1/2 Sheqel, JE5745-AD1984, KM#140, Silver, Denomination/Holyland Sites, Kidron Valley		$16.00
1/2 Sheqel, JE5746-AD1985, KM#152, Silver, Denomination/Holyland Sites, Capernaum		$16.50

	Worn	New
Sheqel, JE5741-45 (1981-85), KM#111, Copper-Nickel, Denomination/Chalice		$0.85
Sheqel, JE5743-AD1982, KM#122, Silver, Denomination/Holyland Sites, Qumran Caves, (proof)		$20.00
Sheqel, JE5744-AD1983, KM#128, Silver, Denomination/Holyland Sites, Herodion Ruins, (proof)		$22.00
Sheqel, JE5743-AD1983, KM#127, Silver, Denomination/Symbols of Valour		$12.50
Sheqel, JE5744-AD1984, KM#135, Silver, Menorah, denomination/Kinsmen		$15.00
Sheqel, JE5745-AD1984, KM#141, Silver, Denomination/Holyland Sites, Kidron Valley, (proof)		$30.00
Sheqel, JE5745-AD1985, KM#155, Silver, Denomination/Ancient ship		$22.00
Sheqel, JE5745-AD1985, KM#148, Silver, Menorah, denomination/Tree		$14.50
Sheqel, JE5746-AD1985, KM#153, Silver, Denomination/Holyland Sites, Capernaum, (proof)		$30.00

Worn   New

5 Sheqalim, JE5742-45 (1982-85), KM#118,
Aluminum-Bronze, Cornucopiae/Denomination $1.50

10 Sheqalim, JE5744 (1984), KM#134, Copper-
Nickel, Ancient Galley/Denomination, Hanukkah $1.50

Worn   New

10 Sheqalim, JE5742-45 (1982-85), KM#119,
Copper-Nickel, Ancient Galley/Denomination $1.25

10 Sheqalim, JE5744 (1984), KM#137,
Copper-Nickel, Theodor Herzl left/Denomination $1.50

*Army Soldiers from the Bravo Company 9th Psyops Battalion, Fort Bragg, N.C., walk off a C-5 Galaxy
from the 9th Airlift Squadron, Dover Air Force Base, Delaware, at the airport of Port-Au-Prince Haiti
on March 13, 2004.*

U.S. AIR FORCE PHOTO BY TECH. SGT. ANDY DUNAWAY

50 Sheqalim, JE5744-45 (1984-85), KM#139,
Aluminum-Bronze, Ancient coin/Denomination

Worn New

$1.50

50 Sheqalim, JE5745 (1985), KM#147,
Aluminum-Bronze, David Ben Guirion left/
Denomination

$1.50

*100 Sheqalim, JE5744-45
(1984-85), KM#143*

	Worn	New
100 Sheqalim, JE5744-45 (1984-85), KM#143, Copper-Nickel, Menorah/Denomination		$2.00
100 Sheqalim, JE5745 (1984), KM#146, Copper-Nickel, Menorah/Denomination, Hanukkah		$2.25
100 Sheqalim, JE5745 (1985), KM#151, Copper-Nickel, Zeev Jabotinsky 3/4 left/Denomination		$2.25
Agorah, JE5745-54 (1985-94), KM#156, Aluminum-Bronze, Ancient ship/Denomination		$0.50

	Worn	New
Agorah, JE5747-52 (1987-92), KM#171, Aluminum-Bronze, Ancient ship/Denomination with Hanukkah legend above		$0.75

	Worn	New
Agorah, JE5748 (1988), KM#193, Aluminum-Bronze, Ancient ship/Denomination with 40th Anniversary legend above		$0.25
5 Agorot, JE5745 (1985), KM#157, Aluminum-Bronze, Ancient coin/Denomination		$0.15

5 Agorot, JE5747-65 (1987-2005), KM#172,
Aluminum-Bronze, Ancient coin/Denomination
with Hanukkah legend above $0.30

5 Agorot, JE5748 (1988), KM#194,
Aluminum-Bronze, Ancient coin/Denomination
with 40th Anniversary legend above $0.50

10 Agorot, JE5745-63 (1985-2003), KM#158,
Aluminum-Bronze, Menorah/Denomination $0.20

10 Agorot, JE5747-65 (1987-2005), KM#173,
Aluminum-Bronze, Menorah/Denomination with
Hanukkah legend above $0.40

10 Agorot, JE5748 (1988), KM#195, Aluminum-
Bronze, Menorah/Denomination with
40th Anniversary legend above $0.50

1/2 New Sheqel, JE5745-64 (1985-2004),
KM#159, Aluminum-Bronze, Denomination/Lyre $0.75

1/2 New Sheqel, JE5746 (1986), KM#167,
Aluminum-Bronze, Denomination/Baron
Edmund de Rothschild $5.00

1/2 New Sheqel, JE5747-AD1986, KM#168,
Silver, Denomination/Holyland Sites - Akko $12.50

10 Agorot, JE5748 (1988),
KM#195

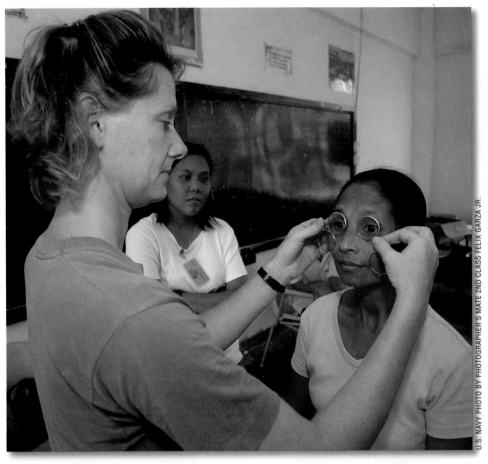

	Worn	New
1/2 New Sheqel, JE5748-AD1987, KM#180, Silver, Denomination/Holyland Sites - Jericho		$13.50

1/2 New Sheqel, JE5747-65 (1987-2005), KM#174, Aluminum-Bronze, Denomination with Hanukkah legend below/Lyre — **$0.85**

	Worn	New
1/2 New Sheqel, JE5749-AD1988, KM#188, Silver, Denomination/Holyland Sites - Caesarea		$15.00

1/2 New Sheqel, JE5748 (1988), KM#196, Aluminum-Bronze, Denomination with 40th Anniversary legend below/Lyre — **$0.85**

1/2 New Sheqel, JE5750-AD1989, KM#202, Silver, Denomination/Holyland Sites - Jaffa Harbor — **$24.00**

	Worn	New
1/2 New Sheqel, JE5755 (1995), KM#304, Copper-Aluminum-Nickel, Denomination/Early American Hanukka lamp		$8.00
1/2 New Sheqel, JE5754 (1994), KM#368, Copper-Aluminum-Nickel, Denomination/Flower		$4.00
1/2 New Sheqel, JE5756 (1996), KM#305, Copper-Aluminum-Nickel, Denomination/ 14th Century French Hanukka lamp		$10.00
1/2 New Sheqel, JE5757 (1997), KM#318, Copper-Aluminum-Nickel, Denomination/ Russian Hanukka lamp		$8.00
1/2 New Sheqel, JE5758 (1998), KM#314, Copper-Aluminum-Nickel, Denomination/ English Hanukka lamp		$8.00

	Worn	New
1/2 New Sheqel, JE5751-AD1990, KM#209, Silver, Denomination/Holyland Sites - Sea of Galilee		$25.00
1/2 New Sheqel, JE5754 (1994), KM#303, Copper-Aluminum-Nickel, Denomination/ Theresienstadt Hanukka lamp		$8.00

US AIR FORCE PHOTO BY: STAFF SGT LEE A OSBERRY JR.

A young girl entranced by the camera hardly notices the pain from a needle as Spc Joshua Swensen, Task Force 163 medical specialist, administers an immunization to her in downtown Kirkuk, Iraq, Aug. 23, 2003. In an effort to support the local communities in Iraq, Coalition Forces utilized 5 separate medical aid teams in different locations to assist physicians in administering various vaccines on the nation's monthly immunization day.

	Worn	New
1/2 New Sheqel, JE5759 (1999), KM#331, Copper-Aluminum-Nickel, Denomination/Menorah		$8.00
1/2 New Sheqel, JE5760 (2000), KM#324, Bronze, Denomination/Mosaic bouquet		$8.00
1/2 New Sheqel, JE5760 (2000), KM#332, Copper-Aluminum-Nickel, Denomination/ Jerusalem Hanukkah lamp		$8.00
1/2 New Sheqel, JE5760 (2000), KM#363, Copper-Aluminum-Nickel, Denomination/Arch		$5.00
1/2 New Sheqel, JE5761 (2001), KM#354, Copper-Aluminum-Nickel, Denomination/ Curacao Hanukka lamp		$8.00
1/2 New Sheqel, JE5762 (2002), KM#389, Copper-Aluminum-Nickel, Denomination/ Polish Hanukka lamp		$8.00
1/2 New Sheqel, JE5762 (2002), KM#355, Copper-Aluminum-Nickel, Denomination/ Yemenite Hanukka lamp		$8.00
1/2 New Sheqel, JE5763 (2003), KM#390, Copper-Aluminum-Nickel, Denomination/ Iraqi Hanukka lamp		$8.00
1/2 New Sheqel, JE5764 (2004), KM#391, Copper-Aluminum-Nickel, Denomination/ Syrian Hanukka lamp		$8.00
New Sheqel, JE5745-54 (1985-94), KM#160, Copper-Nickel, Denomination/Lily		$1.50

	Worn	New
New Sheqel, JE5754-62 (1989-2002), KM#160a, Nickel clad steel, Denomination/Lily		$1.00
New Sheqel, JE5746-AD1985, KM#161, Silver, Denomination, Hanukkah/Ashkenaz lamp (plaque)		$14.00
New Sheqel, JE5746-65 (1986-2005), KM#163, Copper-Nickel, Denomination, Hanukkah/Lily		$2.50
New Sheqel, JE5746-AD1986, KM#164, Silver, Denomination/Artistic symbols		$18.00
New Sheqel, JE5747-AD1986, KM#169, Silver, Denomination/Archways, (proof)		$30.00
New Sheqel, JE5747-AD1987, KM#177, Silver, Denomination/20th Anniversary United Jerusalem		$15.00

Captain Sam Donnelly with the 2-7th Infantry Battalion from Fort Stewart, Georgia, laughs with the children as he hands out diplomas at a grade school graduation ceremony attended by civil affairs representatives from Forward Operating Base Danger in Tikrit, Iraq on May 26, 2005.

New Sheqel, JE5748 (1988), KM#197, Copper-Nickel,
Denomination/Lily

	Worn	New
		$1.75

	Worn	New
New Sheqel, JE5748-AD1987, KM#181, Silver, Denomination/Holyland Sites, Jericho, (proof)		$30.00
New Sheqel, JE5748-AD1988, KM#185, Silver, Denomination/40th with council		$13.50
New Sheqel, JE5749-AD1988, KM#189, Silver, Denomination/Holyland Sites, Caesarea, (proof)		$40.00

New Sheqel, JE5748 (1988), KM#198,
Copper-Nickel, Denomination/Bust of Maimonides $1.75

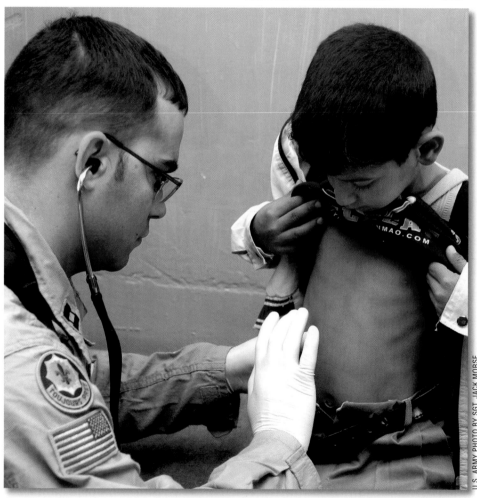

Capt. Jason Seery, a doctor with 2nd Armored Cavalry Regiment in Baghdad, examines a young Iraqi boy during a medical assistance mission near Balad, Iraq, Dec. 7, 2003. The 308th Civil Affairs Brigade, out of Homewood, Ill., facilitates the missions, which involve doctors, medics and translators, every Sunday in the Balad area. The soldiers are deployed in support of Operation Iraqi Freedom.

	Worn	New
New Sheqel, JE5749-AD1989, KM#199, Silver, Denomination/Deer in forest		$22.00
New Sheqel, JE5750-AD1990, KM#212, Silver, Denomination/Menorah, archaeology		$25.00
New Sheqel, JE5751-AD1990, KM#215, Silver, Denomination/Cochin lamp, Hanukkah		$25.00
New Sheqel, JE5751-AD1991, KM#218, Silver, Denomination/Airplane, immigrants		$20.00
New Sheqel, JE5752-AD1992, KM#225, Silver, Denomination/Balance scales, Israeli law		$40.00
New Sheqel, JE5753-AD1993, KM#240, Silver, Denomination/Tourism - key, sailboat, sun and columns		$25.00
New Sheqel, JE5753-AD1993, KM#247, Silver, Denomination/Star and flames, Revolt and Heroism		$25.00
5 New Sheqalim, JE5750-62 (1990-2002), KM#207, Copper-Nickel, Denomination/ Ancient column		$3.75

5 New Sheqalim, JE5750-62 (1990-2002), KM#207

	Worn	New
5 New Sheqalim, JE5750-AD2004, KM#208, Copper-Nickel, Denomination/Levi Eshkol facing		$5.00

	Worn	New
5 New Sheqalim, JE5751-65 (1991-2005), KM#217, Copper-Nickel, Denomination, Hannukah/Ancient column		$4.00

	Worn	New
5 New Sheqalim, JE5753-AD1993, KM#237, Copper-Nickel, Denomination/Chaim Weizmann facing		$5.00
10 New Sheqalim, JE5755-62 (1995-2002), KM#270, Bronze with Nickel bonded steel, ring Denomination/ Palmtree and baskets		$7.00
10 New Sheqalim, JE5755 (1995), KM#273, Bronze with Nickel bonded steel, ring Denomination/Golda Meir		$10.00
10 New Sheqalim, JE5756-65 (1996-2005), KM#315, Bronze with Nickel bonded steel, ring Denomination, Hannukah/Palm Tree and baskets		$8.00

Children come in droves when they see U.S. soldiers from the 39th Infantry Brigade on a foot patrol, through the village of Al Asyria, near Taji, Iraq, on July 16, 2004.

Jordan

	Worn	New
Fils, AH1398-1406 (1978-85), KM#35, Bronze, Bust right/Date and denomination	$0.10	$0.50

10 Fils, AH1398-1409 (1978-89), KM#37

	Worn	New
5 Fils, AH1398-1406 (1978-85), KM#36, Bronze, Bust right/Date and denomination	$0.10	$0.30
10 Fils, AH1398-1409 (1978-89), KM#37, Bronze, Bust right/Date and denomination	$0.10	$0.40

	Worn	New
25 Fils, AH1398-1411 (1978-91), KM#38, Copper-Nickel, Bust right/Date and denomination	$0.20	$0.75

	Worn	New
50 Fils, AH1398-1411 (1978-91), KM#39, Copper-Nickel, Bust right/Date and denomination	$0.25	$1.25

	Worn	New
1/4 Dinar, AH1398-1406 (1978-85), KM#41, Copper-Nickel, Bust right/Tree	$0.75	$4.00
1/2 Dinar, AH1400 (1980), KM#42, Copper-Nickel, 3/4 Bust right/Branch and Mosques	$1.50	$5.00
Dinar, AH1406 (1985), KM#47, Nickel-Bronze, Bust right in circle/Crown above sun		$7.50
1/2 Qirsh, AH1416 (1996), KM#60, Copper plated steel, Bust left/Denomination	$0.30	$0.65

	Worn	New
100 Fils, AH1398-1411 (1978-91), KM#40, Copper-Nickel, Bust right/Date and denomination	$0.40	$2.00

1/2 Dinar, AH1400 (1980), KM#42

A US Army CH-47 helicopter flies over Baghdad, Iraq, during a distinguished visitor flight in support of Operation Iraqi Freedom, July 20, 2003.

	Worn	New
Qirsh, AH1414-16 (1994-96), KM#56, Bronze plated steel, Bust left/Denomination	$0.40	$1.25
1 1/2 Piastres, AH1412-16 (1992-96), KM#53, Stainless steel, Bust left/Denomination	$0.65	$1.50
5 Piastres, AH1412-18 (1992-98), KM#54, Nickel plated steel, Bust left/Denomination	$0.75	$2.00
10 Piastres, AH1412-16 (1992-96), KM#55, Nickel plated steel, Bust left/Denomination	$1.00	$2.25
1/4 Dinar, AH1416-17 (1996-97), KM#61, Nickel-Brass, Bust left/Denomination		$3.00

1/4 Dinar, AH1416-17 (1996-97), KM#61

	Worn	New
1/2 Dinar, AH1416 (1996), KM#58, Brass, Bust left/Denomination		$4.00
1/2 Dinar, AH1417 (1997), KM#63, Aluminum-Bronze, Bust left/Denomination		$8.00
Dinar, AH1415 (1995), KM#62, Brass, Bust left/Denomination, FAO		$10.00
Dinar, AH1416-17 (1996-97), KM#59, Brass, Bust left/Denomination		$8.00
Dinar, AH1419 (1998), KM#64, Brass, Bust left/Denomination		$5.50
Dinar, AH1419 (1998), KM#65, Brass, Bust left/Denomination		$7.00
5 Dinars, ND(1995), KM#57, Copper-Nickel, Bust left/Denomination, Flowers		$10.00
Qirsh, AH1421 (2000), KM#78, Copper plated steel, Bust right/denomination		$1.00
5 Piastres, AH1421 (2000), KM#73, Nickel clad steel, Bust right/denomination		$2.00
10 Piastres, AH1421 (2000), KM#74, Nickel clad steel, Bust right/denomination		$4.00
1/2 Dinar, AH1421 (2000), KM#79, Copper-Nickel center with Brass ring, Bust right/denomination		$6.00
3 Dinars, AH1423-AD2002, KM#75, Brass, Bust facing/Building		$40.00
5 Dinars, AH1420-AD2000, KM#71, Brass, Bust facing/Scene in River		$20.00

Veterinary Technician Spc. Destiny Morgan performs a periodic check-up on Falla, an Air Force military working dog, Jan. 16, 2004, at Tallil Air Base, Iraq. Morgan is the only veterinary technician in the theater and takes care of the Air Force military working dogs on Tallil at Kirkuk Air Base.

Kuwait

	Worn	New
Fils, AH1382-1408 (1962-88), KM#9, Nickel-Brass, Denomination/Ship and date	$0.15	$0.50
5 Fils, AH1382-1415 (1962-95), KM#10, Nickel-Brass, Denomination/Ship and date	$0.10	$0.40

	Worn	New
10 Fils, AH1382-1410 (1962-90), KM#11, Nickel-Brass, Denomination/Ship and date	$0.15	$0.75
20 Fils, AH1382-1417 (1962-97), KM#12, Copper-Nickel, Denomination/Ship and date	$0.20	$1.25
20 Fils, AH1421 (2001), KM#12c, Stainless steel, Denomination/Ship and date		$1.00
50 Fils, AH1382-1415 (1962-95), KM#13, Copper-Nickel, Denomination/Ship and date	$0.25	$1.35

	Worn	New
100 Fils, AH1382-1415 (1962-95), KM#14, Copper-Nickel, Denomination/Ship and date	$0.50	$1.75
2 Dinars, ND(1976), KM#15, Silver, Two men/ Oil equipment		$45.00

2 Dinars, ND(1976), KM#15

Spc. Darren McCrae (right) of Troop B, 2nd Squadron, 14th Cavalry Regiment, 1st Brigade, 25th Infantry Division (Stryker Brigade Combat Team) and Capt. Keith Walters (left), Troop B commander, hand out backpacks to schoolchildren in the village of Tal Banat, Iraq, December 8. The cavalry Soldiers handed out backpacks while a civil affairs team worked with local leaders to make an assessment of possible projects to assist the residents of the area.

U.S. ARMY PHOTO BY SPC. BLAIR LARSON

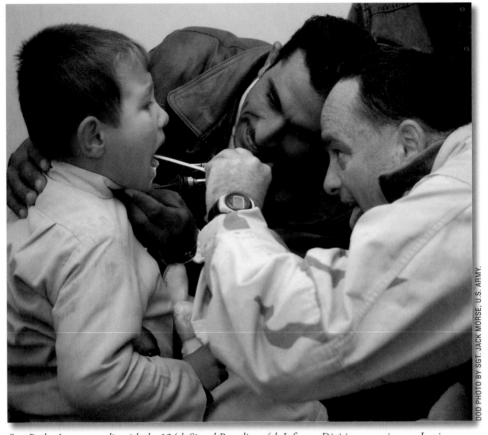

Spc. Rocky Amez, a medic with the 124th Signal Battalion, 4th Infantry Division, examines an Iraqi boy during a medical assessment visit to a school near Balad, Iraq, Dec. 28, 2003. Doctors, medics, and additional military personnel from several units visited the school to assess student's medical needs.

Lebanon

	Worn	New
5 Piastres, 1968-70, KM#25.1, Nickel-Brass, Tree and date/Denomination in wreath	$0.10	$0.25
5 Piastres, 1972-80, KM#25.2, Nickel-Brass, Tree and date/Revised denomination in wreath	$0.10	$0.15

	Worn	New
25 Piastres, 1968-75, KM#27.1, Nickel-Brass, Tree and date/Denomination in wreath	$0.15	$0.40

	Worn	New
10 Piastres, 1968-75, KM#26, Nickel-Brass, Tree and date/Denomination in wreath	$0.10	$0.45

	Worn	New
25 Piastres, 1980, KM#27.2, Nickel-Brass, Tree and date/Revised denomination in wreath	$0.15	$0.30

	Worn	New
50 Piastres, 1968-78, KM#28.1, Nickel, Tree and date/Denomination in wreath	$0.25	$0.50
50 Piastres, 1980, KM#28.2, Nickel, Tree and date/Revised denomination in wreath	$0.25	$0.50

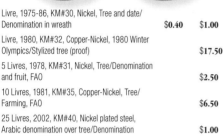

	Worn	New
Livre, 1975-86, KM#30, Nickel, Tree and date/Denomination in wreath	$0.40	$1.00
Livre, 1980, KM#32, Copper-Nickel, 1980 Winter Olympics/Stylized tree (proof)		$17.50
5 Livres, 1978, KM#31, Nickel, Tree/Denomination and fruit, FAO		$2.50
10 Livres, 1981, KM#35, Copper-Nickel, Tree/ Farming, FAO		$6.50
25 Livres, 2002, KM#40, Nickel plated steel, Arabic denomination over tree/Denomination		$1.00

	Worn	New
50 Livres, 1996, KM#37, Stainless steel, Arabic denomination over tree/Denomination		$1.00
100 Livres, 1995-2000, KM#38, Copper-Zinc Arabic denomination over tree/Denomination		$1.50
250 Livres, 1995-2000, KM#36, Brass, Arabic denomination over tree/Denomination		$2.00
500 llvres, 1995-2000, KM#39, Stainless steel, Arabic denomination over tree/Denomination		$2.50

50 Piastres, 1968-78, KM#28.1

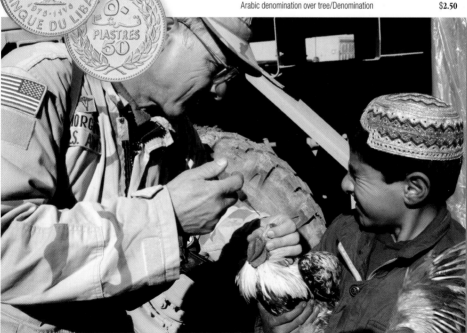

U.S. ARMY PHOTO BY SPC. GUL A ALISAN

Col. Earl Morgan, a veterinarian with Combined Joint Civil Military Operation Task Force (CJCMOTF) Headquarters (HHC), Bagram, gives dewormer medicine to a chicken during a Medical Assistance Mission held by CJCMOTF Civil Affairs team in the Roza Sharif village clinic, Ghazni, Afghanistan, Feb. 13, 2004. Soldiers are in Afghanistan in support of Operation Enduring Freedom.

An Afghan boy holds up a teddy bear given to him by Airmen of the 455th Air Expeditionary Wing at nearby Bagram Air Base during an adopt-a-village visit. The program allows Airmen to assist villages in Afghanistan with infrastructure, fresh water, school supplies and toys for children.

Oman

	Worn	New
5 Baisa, AH1395-1410 (1975-89), KM#50, Bronze, Crossed sword Arms/Denomination	$0.10	$0.45
10 Baisa, AH1395 (1975), KM#51, Bronze, Two palm trees/Denomination	$0.15	$0.65
10 Baisa, AH1395-1418 (1975-97), KM#52.1, Bronze, Crossed sword Arms/Denomination	$0.15	$0.65
10 Baisa, AH1420-AD1999, KM#52.2, Bronze, clad steel, Crossed sword Arms/Denomination	$0.15	$0.65
25 Baisa, AH 1395-1418 (1975-97), KM#45a, Copper-Nickel, Crossed sword Arms/Denomination	$0.20	$0.85

	Worn	New
50 Baisa, AH 1395-1418 (1975-97), KM#46a, Copper-Nickel, Crossed sword Arms/Denomination	$0.30	$1.50
100 Baisa, AH1404-AD1983, KM#68, Copper-Nickel, Crossed sword Arms/Denomination	$0.40	$2.25
1/4 Omani Rial, AH1400-AD1980, KM#66, Aluminum-Bronze, Crossed sword Arms/ Denomination	$0.50	$1.00

50 Baisa, AH 1395-1418 (1975-97), KM#46a

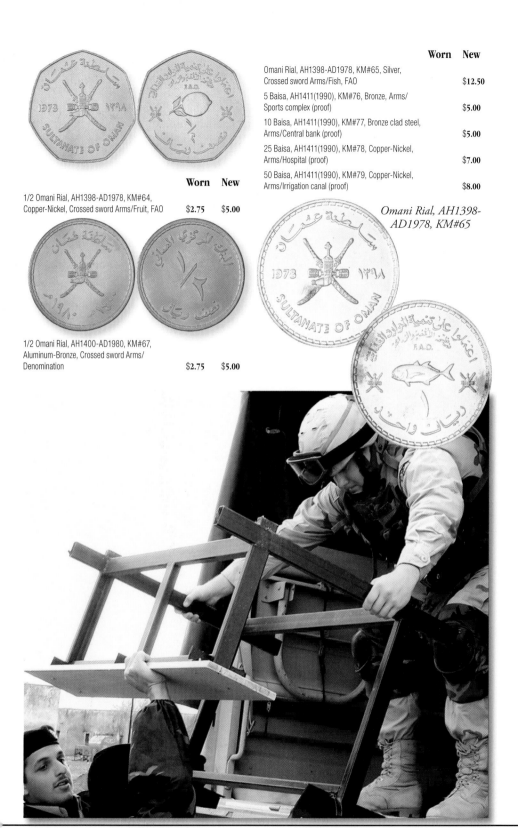

1/2 Omani Rial, AH1398-AD1978, KM#64,
Copper-Nickel, Crossed sword Arms/Fruit, FAO

1/2 Omani Rial, AH1400-AD1980, KM#67,
Aluminum-Bronze, Crossed sword Arms/
Denomination

	Worn	New
1/2 Omani Rial, AH1398-AD1978, KM#64, Copper-Nickel, Crossed sword Arms/Fruit, FAO	$2.75	$5.00
1/2 Omani Rial, AH1400-AD1980, KM#67, Aluminum-Bronze, Crossed sword Arms/Denomination	$2.75	$5.00

	Worn	New
Omani Rial, AH1398-AD1978, KM#65, Silver, Crossed sword Arms/Fish, FAO		$12.50
5 Baisa, AH1411(1990), KM#76, Bronze, Arms/Sports complex (proof)		$5.00
10 Baisa, AH1411(1990), KM#77, Bronze clad steel, Arms/Central bank (proof)		$5.00
25 Baisa, AH1411(1990), KM#78, Copper-Nickel, Arms/Hospital (proof)		$7.00
50 Baisa, AH1411(1990), KM#79, Copper-Nickel, Arms/Irrigation canal (proof)		$8.00

*Omani Rial, AH1398-
AD1978, KM#65*

	Worn	New
100 Baisa, AH1411(1990), KM#80, Copper-Nickel, Arms/University (proof)		$10.00
2 Omani Rials, AH1411(1990), KM#81, Silver, Arms/Bust (proof)		$50.00
100 Baisa, AH1411-AD1991, KM#82, Aluminum-Bronze, with Copper-Nickel ring, Arms/Scene		$5.00

	Worn	New
5 Baisa, AH1420-AD1999, KM#150, Bronze clad steel, Arms/Denomination		$0.50
10 Baisa, AH1420-AD1999, KM#151, Bronze clad steel, Arms/Denomination		$0.75

	Worn	New
25 Baisa, AH1420-AD1999, KM#152, Copper-Nickel, Arms/Denomination		$1.00
50 Baisa, AH1420-AD1999, KM#153, Copper-Nickel, Arms/Denomination		$1.75
10 Baisa, ND(1995), KM#94, Bronze clad steel, Arms and denomination/FAO 50th		$1.25
Omani Rial, ND(1995), KM#96, Silver, Arms and denomination/FAO 50th		$30.00

50 Baisa, AH1420-AD1999, KM#153

MAJ Lawendowski from the Alaskan National Guard, assembles a swing set for Iraqi children living in an impoverished nighborhood, during a joint patrole / humanitarian aid mission, in the town of Al Hillah, Iraq on May 14 2005.

U.S. ARMY PHOTO BY SGT HAMILTON, ARTHUR

	Worn	New
50 Baisa, ND(1995), KM#95, Copper-Nickel, Arms/ United Nations 50th		$3.00
Omani Rial, ND(1995), KM#145, Silver, Arms/ United Nations 50th (proof)		$40.00

Pakistan

	Worn	New
Paisa, 1974-79, KM#33, Aluminum, Crescent over spire/Denomination and cotton plants, FAO	$0.20	$0.75

	Worn	New
2 Paisa, 1974-76, KM#34, Aluminum, Crescent over spire/Denomination and rice plants, FAO	$0.35	$1.00

	Worn	New
5 Paisa, 1974-81, KM#35, Aluminum, Crescent over spire/Denomination and sugar cane plants, FAO	$0.35	$1.00

	Worn	New
10 Paisa, 1974-81, KM#36, Aluminum, Crescent over spire/Denomination and wheat ears, FAO	$0.35	$1.00

5 Paisa, 1974-81, KM#35

	Worn	New
25 Paisa, 1975-81, KM#37, Copper-Nickel, Crescent over spire/Denomination over plant	$0.35	$1.00

	Worn	New
50 Paisa, 1976, KM#39, Copper-Nickel, Denomination in circles/Bust facing	$0.50	$1.50

	Worn	New
50 Paisa, 1975-81, KM#38, Copper-Nickel, Crescent over spire/Denomination	$0.35	$1.00

	Worn	New
Rupee, 1977, KM#45, Copper-Nickel, Spire/ Islamic Summit	$0.75	$2.00

U.S. and Romanian troops from Kandahar Army Airfield Afghanistan conduct a Combined Medical Assistance exercise mission where members of the 486th Civil Affairs, 308th Tactical Psychological Operations Company, 10th Mountain Police Company and C Med 10th Mountain Forward Support Battalion visit the village of Loy Karezak to provide the villagers with medical care and distribute food supplies. Here registered nurse 1st Lt. Dawn Dirksen of 9-11th Forward Surgical Team checks a young girls throat.

	Worn	New
100 Rupees, 1977, KM#48, Silver, Denomination and date/ Head rests on hand		$30.00
150 Rupees, 1976, KM#42, Silver, Crescent over spire/Gavial crocodile		$37.50

	Worn	New
Rupee, 1977, KM#46, Copper-Nickel, Denomination and date/Head rests on hand	$0.75	$2.00
Rupee, 1979-81, KM#57.1, Copper-Nickel, Star and crescent/Denomination	$0.40	$1.15
100 Rupees, 1976, KM#40, Silver, Crescent over spire/Tropogan pheasant		$30.00
100 Rupees, ND(1976), KM#41, Silver, Star and Crescent/Bust facing		$30.00
100 Rupees, 1977, KM#47, Silver, Date and legends/ Spire, Islamic Summit		$30.00

	Worn	New
5 Paisa, 1981-92, KM#52, Aluminum, Crescent over date/Denomination and sugar cane plants	$0.35	$1.00

50 Baisa, AH1420-AD1999, KM#153

Staff Sergeant Jen Brooks of Kandahar Provincial Reconstruction Team (PRT) hands a student from Abdul Ahad Karzai Middle School in Kahdahar City a piece of candy during the unit's assessment of the school, September 14, 2004. The Kandahar PRT is providing humanitarian aid in Afghanistan to support Operation Enduring Freedom.

50 Paisa, AH1401 (1981), KM#51, Copper-Nickel, Star and crescent/Hejira

	Worn	New
	$0.75	$2.00

Worn   New

10 Paisa, 1981-93, KM#53, Aluminum, Crescent over date/Denomination $0.35 $1.00

Rupee, 1981-90, KM#57.2, Copper-Nickel, Star and crescent/Denomination $0.35 $1.00

50 Paisa, 1981-96, KM#54, Copper-Nickel, Star and crescent/Denomination $0.35 $1.00

*50 Paisa, AH1401
(1981), KM#51*

Rupee, AH1401 (1981), KM#55, Copper-Nickel, Star and crescent/Hejira $0.75 $2.50

US and Romanian troops from Kandahar Army Airfield, Afghanistan visited the village of Kalagai to offer medical assistance and provide humanitarian aid to the villagers during a Combined Medical Assistance Exercise (CMAX). Private First Class Jeremy Edwards with the 6th/12th Quartermaster out of Fort Bragg, North Carolina helps one of the villagers unload food that will be distributed within the village of Kalagai.

	Worn	New
Rupee, 1981, KM#56, Copper-Nickel, Star and crescent/World Food Day, FAO	$0.75	$3.00
Rupee, 1998-2004, KM#62, Bronze, Bust left/ Mosque	$0.25	$0.65
2 Rupees, 1998, KM#63, Nickel-Brass, Star and crescent/Mosque	$0.30	$0.85
2 Rupees, 1999-2004, KM#64, Nickel-Brass Star and crescent/Mosque, clouds above	$0.30	$0.85
5 Rupees, 1995, KM#59, Copper, Star and crescent/ United Nations, 50th		$5.50

5 Rupees, 1995, KM#59

	Worn	New
5 Rupees, 2002-04, KM#65, Copper-Nickel, Star and crescent/Denomination	$1.00	$3.00
10 Rupees, 1998, KM#61, Copper-Nickel, Star and crescent/Pakistan Senate, 25th	$3.50	$6.50
10 Rupees, 2003, KM#66, Copper-Nickel, Star and crescent/Flowers	$3.50	$6.50

	Worn	New
50 Rupees, 1997, KM#60, Copper-Nickel, Star and Crescent/Flag above dates	$3.50	$7.50

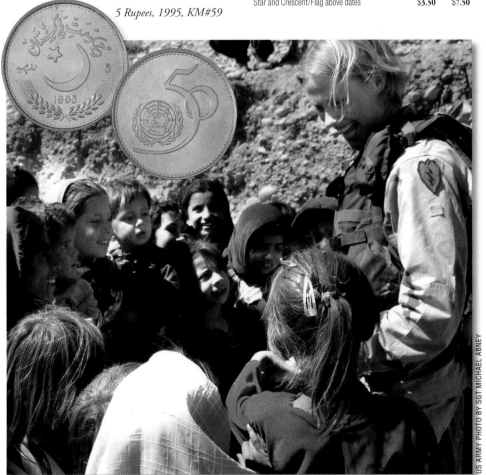

SPC Stevens of Task Force Pirate mingle with the children of Jagdelak during the Humanitarian Aid Mission in Afghanistain.

	Worn	New
Dirham, AH1393-AD1973, KM#2, Bronze, Denomination/Sailboat and palm trees	$0.10	$0.60

	Worn	New
50 Dirhams, AH1393-1419-AD1973-98, KM#5, Copper-Nickel, Denomination/Sailboat and palm trees	$0.40	$2.25
25 Dirhams, AH1421-AD2000, KM#8, Copper-Nickel, Denomination/Sailboat and palm trees		$1.50
50 Dirhams, AH1421-24-AD2000-02, KM#9, Copper-Nickel, Denomination/Sailboat and palm trees		$2.00

	Worn	New
5 Dirhams, AH1393-98-AD1973-78, KM#3, Bronze, Denomination/Sailboat and palm trees	$0.10	$0.75
10 Dirhams, AH1392-93-AD1972-73, KM#1, Bronze, Denomination/Sailboat and palm trees	$0.50	$2.50

10 Dirhams, AH1392-93-AD1972-73, KM#1

	Worn	New
25 Dirhams, AH1393-1421-AD1973-2000, KM#4, Copper-Nickel, Denomination/Sailboat and palm trees	$0.25	$1.75

A soldier from Charlie Company, 2/108th Infantry Regiment shakes hands with a little Iraqi child while his mother watches, during a joint patrol with the Iraqi National Guard (ING) in the village of Tartar near Samarra, Iraq on 6 Sept 04. C Co, 2/108th INF and ING conducts these missions to help deter criminal activity against Coalition Forces. C Co, 2/108th INF is in Iraq supporting Operation Iraqi Freedom.

US ARMY PHOTO BY SGT. APRIL L. JOHNSON

Pfc. Tyson Byram, with the 10th Mountain Forward Support Battalion, marks a child's hand after he was seen by the medical staff in the village of Kalagai, Afghanistan, Sept. 24, 2003. U.S. and Romanian soldiers from Kandahar Army Airfield visited the village to offer medical assistance and provide humanitarian aid during a Combined Medical Assistance Exercise.

DOD PHOTO BY PFC. HUGO A. BARAY-VASQUEZ, U.S. ARMY.

Saudi Arabia

	Worn	New
5 Halala, AH1397(1976)-AH1400 (1979), KM#53, Copper-Nickel, Crossed swords below palm/ Denomination and date	$0.25	$2.00

	Worn	New
5 Halala, AH1398 (1977), KM#57, Copper-Nickel, Crossed swords below palm/Denomination and date	$0.30	$1.00

	Worn	New
5 Halala, AH1408 (1987), KM#61, Copper-Nickel, Crossed swords below palm/ Denomination and date	$0.30	$1.00

	Worn	New
10 Halala, AH1397 (1976)-AH1400 (1979), KM#54, Copper-Nickel, Crossed swords below palm/ Denomination and date	$0.75	$3.00

Worn	New
25 Halala, AH1397 (1976)-AH1400 (1979), KM#55, Copper-Nickel, Crossed swords below palm/ Denomination and date	$0.50	$3.00

Worn	New
10 Halala, AH1398 (1977), KM#58, Copper-Nickel, Crossed swords below palm/Denomination and date	$0.25	$1.00

25 Halala, AH1408 (1987)-AH1423 (2002), KM#63, Copper-Nickel, Crossed swords below palm/ Denomination and date | $0.40 | $1.50

10 Halala, AH1408 (1987)-AH1423 (2002), Copper-Nickel, Crossed swords below palm/ Denomination and date | $0.30 | $1.25

25 Halala, AH1397 (1976)- AH1400 (1979), KM#55

Pvt. Jeremy Wilson with 10th Mountain Military Police (MP) Company hands a stick of gum to one of the children in the village of Haji Mohammad Zai Kalacha.

Worn   New

50 Halala, AH1397 (1976)-AH1400 (1979), KM#56,
Copper-Nickel, Crossed swords below palm/
enomination and date $0.75 $3.50

50 Halala, AH1408 (1987)-AH1423 (2002), KM#64,
Copper-Nickel, Crossed swords below palm/
Denomination and date $0.50 $3.50

*100 Halala, AH1396
(1976)-AH1400 (1980),
KM#52*

Worn   New

100 Halala, AH1396 (1976)-AH1400 (1980), KM#52,
Copper-Nickel, Crossed swords below palm/
Denomination and date $0.65 $3.50

100 Halala, AH1397-AD1977, KM#59,
Copper-Nickel, Crossed swords below palm, dates/
Denomination, FAO $225.00

100 Halala, AH1398-AD1978, KM#59,
Copper-Nickel, Crossed swords below palm, dates/
Denomination, FAO $0.75 $3.50

100 Halala, AH1408 (1987)-AH1414 (1993), KM#65,
Copper-Nickel, Crossed swords below palm/
Denomination and date $1.00 $4.00

Master Sgt. Robert Copeland assigned to 36th Information Operation Command, Austin, Texas, holds an Afghan flag while an Afhan boy holds an American flag in his brand new wheelchair. The Wheelchair was distribute by the Wheelchair Foundation to physically disabled Afghan, man, woman and children at a compound in Kubal, Afghanistan, Sept. 22, 2003.

	Worn	New
100 Halala, AH1419 (1999), KM#66, Brass in Copper-Nickel ring, Crossed swords below palm/Denomination and date	$1.00	$5.00
100 Halala, AH1419 (1999), KM#67, Brass in Copper-Nickel ring, Palm on base/Denomination and date	$1.50	$6.50

Somalia

	Worn	New
5 Senti, 1976, KM#24, Aluminum, Arms and legend/Food, FAO	$0.10	$0.35

	Worn	New
10 Senti, 1976, KM#25, Aluminum, Arms and legend/Sheep, FAO	$0.10	$0.50

	Worn	New
50 Senti, 1976, KM#26, Copper-Nickel, Arms and legend/Food, FAO	$0.15	$0.75
50 Senti, 1984, KM#26a, Nickel plated steel, Arms and legend/Food, FAO	$1.00	$5.00

	Worn	New
Shilling, 1976, KM#27, Copper-Nickel, Arms and legend/Sheep, FAO	$0.35	$2.25
Shilling, 1984, KM#27a, Nickel plated steel, Arms and legend/Sheep, FAO	$2.00	$10.00
10 Shillings, ND(1979), KM#28, Copper-Nickel, Arms and legend/Workers		$7.00

Worn **New**

10 Shillings, ND(1979), KM#29, Copper-Nickel,
Arms and legend/Tents and people   **$7.00**

10 Shillings, ND(1979), KM#30, Copper-Nickel,
Arms and legend/Lab workers   **$7.00**

10 Shillings,
ND(1979), KM#28

Sergeant Michael Loston, of Comanche Company 1-23 Infantry, 3rd Brigade, 2nd Infantry Division Stryker Brigade Combat Team (SBCT), hands a girl some glue, at a school in Mosul, Iraq on May 15, 2004. C Co. are handing school supplies out to the children at the school in Mosul. 3rd Bde. SBCT is in Iraq in support of Operation Iraqi Freedom.

	Worn	New
10 Shillings, ND(1979), KM#31, Copper-Nickel,
Arms and legend/Dancers | | $7.00

	Worn	New
10 Shillings, ND(1979), KM#32, Copper-Nickel,
Arms and legend/Man and woman | | $7.00

	Worn	New
25 Shillings, ND(1984), KM#40, Copper-Nickel, Arms and legend/Sea turtle		$35.00
5 Shilling/Scellini, 2000, KM#45, Aluminum, Arms and denomination/Elephant		$1.50
10 Shillings, 2000, KM#90, Nickel clad steel, Arms and denomination/Rat		$1.25
10 Shillings, 2000, KM#91, Nickel clad steel, Arms and denomination/Ox		$1.25
10 Shillings, 2000, KM#92, Nickel clad steel, Arms and denomination/Tiger		$1.25
10 Shillings, 2000, KM#93, Nickel clad steel, Arms and denomination/Rabbit		$1.25

25 Shillings, ND(1984), KM#40

	Worn	New
10 Shillings, 2000, KM#94, Nickel clad steel, Arms and denomination/Dragon		$1.50
10 Shillings, 2000, KM#95, Nickel clad steel, Arms and denomination/Snake		$1.25
10 Shillings, 2000, KM#96, Nickel clad steel, Arms and denomination/Horse		$1.25
10 Shillings, 2000, KM#97, Nickel clad steel, Arms and denomination/Goat		$1.25

	Worn	New
10 Shillings, 2000, KM#98, Nickel clad steel, Arms and denomination/Monkey		$1.25
10 Shillings, 2000, KM#99, Nickel clad steel, Arms and denomination/Rooster		$1.25
10 Shillings, 2000, KM#100, Nickel clad steel, Arms and denomination/Dog		$1.25
10 Shillings, 2000, KM#101, Nickel clad steel, Arms and denomination/Pig		$1.25
10 Shillings/Scellini, 2000, KM#46, Aluminum, Arms and denomination/Camel, FAO		$2.00
25 Shillings, 2001, KM#103, Brass, Arms and denomination/Soccer player		$1.25

Worn	New
50 Shillings, 2002, KM#111, Nickel clad steel, Arms and denomination/Mandrill	$0.85
100 Shillings, 2002, KM#112, Brass, Arms and denomination/Queen of Sheba	$3.50

Somaliland

	Worn	New
Shilling, 1994, KM#1, Aluminum, Bird/Denomination		$3.00
5 Shillings, 2002, KM#4, Aluminum, Denomination/ Sir Richart F. Burton		$1.50

10 Shillings, 2002, KM#3

Staff Sgt. James Partin talks to local children during an Operation Kaleidoscope mission recently. The new program adds extra protection to perimeter defense procedures and gives locals a point of contact to call if they see suspicious activity that could harm U.S. or coalitions forces. Sergeant Partin is assigned to the 407th Expeditionary Security Forces Squadron at nearby Tallil Air Base.

	Worn	New
5 Shillings, 2002, KM#5, Aluminum, Rooster/ Denomination		$1.00
10 Shillings, 2002, KM#3, Brass, Vervet monkey/ Denomination		$0.75
20 Shillings, 2002, KM#6, Stainless Steel, Geryhound dog/Denomination		$3.00
1000 Shillings, 2002, KM#2, Silver, Arms/ Sir Richard F. Burton		$35.00

Sudan

![coin]

	Worn	New
5 Millim, AH1395-98-AD1975-78, KM#54a.1, Brass, Denomination/Arms	$0.15	$0.40

![coin]

	Worn	New
5 Millim, AH1396-98-AD1976-78, KM#60, Brass, Denomination/Small Arms, FAO		$0.20

	Worn	New
5 Millim, AH1396-AD1976, KM#94, Brass, Denomination/Arms, legend above		$0.25
5 Millim, AH1398-AD1978, KM#54a.2, Brass, Denomination/Arms, long ribbon above		$0.40
5 Millim, AH1400-AD1980, KM#54a.3, Brass, Denomination/Arms, short ribbon above (proof)		$1.00
10 Millim, AH1395-98-AD1975-78, KM#55a.1, Brass, Denomination/Arms, short ribbon	$0.25	$1.00
10 Millim, AH1398-AD1978, KM#55a.2, Brass, Denomination/Arms, long ribbon	$0.75	$4.25
10 Millim, AH1400-AD1980, KM#55a.3, Brass, Denomination, fine legend/Arms, short ribbon	$0.25	$1.00

![coin]

	Worn	New
10 Millim, AH1396-98-AD1976-78, KM#61, Brass, Denomination/Small Arms, date below	$0.10	$0.25
10 Millim, AH1396-AD1976, KM#62, Brass, Denomination/Small Arms divide dates	$0.10	$0.40
10 Millim, AH1400-AD1980, KM#111, Brass, Denomination/ Arms with long ribbon	$1.25	$7.50
Ghirsh, AH1403-AD1983, KM#97, Brass, Denomination/Arms	$0.25	$2.00

	Worn	New
2 Ghirsh, AH1395-98-AD1975-78, KM#57.1, Copper-Nickel, Denomination/Arms	$0.20	$0.75

2 Ghirsh, AH1398-1400-AD1978-80, KM#57.2, Copper-Nickel, Denomination/Arms with long ribbon	$0.20	$0.75
2 Ghirsh, AH1403-AD1983, KM#57.2a, Brass, Denomination, revised legend/Arms	$0.75	$3.50

2 Ghirsh, AH1396-98-AD1976-78, KM#63.1

	Worn	New
2 Ghirsh, AH1399-1400-AD1979-80, KM#57.3, Copper-Nickel, Thin denomination and legend/Arms	$0.20	$0.75
2 Ghirsh, AH1396-98-AD1976-78, KM#63.1, Copper-Nickel, Thick denomination/Arms in wheat ears	$0.20	$0.75
2 Ghirsh, AH1398-AD1978, KM#63.2, Copper-Nickel, Thin denomination/Arms in wheat ears	$5.00	$10.00
2 Ghirsh, AH1396-AD1976, KM#64, Copper-Nickel, Denomination/Arms long legend above	$0.20	$0.60

5 Ghirsh, AH1395-AD1975, KM#58.1, Copper-Nickel, Denomination/Arms	$0.25	$0.85
5 Ghirsh, AH1400-AD1980, KM#58.2, Copper-Nickel, Denomination/Arms, long ribbon above	$0.25	$0.85
5 Ghirsh, AH1397-1400-AD1977-80, KM#58.3, Copper-Nickel, Denomination, fine legend/Arms	$0.25	$0.85
5 Ghirsh, AH1400-AD1980, KM#58.4, Copper-Nickel, Denomination, large legend/Arms, long ribbon	$0.25	$0.85

	Worn	New
5 Ghirsh, AH1396-98-AD1976-78, KM#65, Copper-Nickel, Denomination/Arms in wheat ears, FAO	$0.20	$0.65

	Worn	New
5 Ghirsh, AH1396-AD1976, KM#66, Copper-Nickel, Denomination/Arms long legend above	$0.25	$1.00
5 Ghirsh, AH1398-AD1978, KM#74, Copper-Nickel, Clasped hands, Arab Economic Unity/Arms	$0.15	$0.50
5 Ghirsh, Ah1401-AD1981, KM#84, Copper-Nickel, Cow and calf, FAO/Arms	$0.20	$0.75
5 Ghirsh, AH1403-AD1983, KM#110.1, Brass, Denomination/Arms	$0.25	$1.50

	Worn	New
5 Ghirsh, AH1403-AD1983, KM#110.2, Brass, Denomination/Arms, long ribbon	$0.50	$2.25
5 Ghirsh, AH1403-AD1983, KM#110.3, Brass, Fine denomiantion and legend/Arms	$5.00	$10.00
5 Ghirsh, AH1403-AD1983, KM#110.4, Brass, Large denomination and legend/Arms, long ribbon	$1.50	$7.50

	Worn	New
10 Ghirsh, AH1395-AD1975, KM#59.1, Copper-Nickel, Denomination/Arms	$0.50	$2.50
10 Ghirsh, AH1400-AD1980, KM#59.2, Copper-Nickel, Denomination/Arms, long ribbon	$0.50	$2.50
10 Ghirsh, AH1403-AD1983, KM#59.3, Copper-Nickel, Denomination/Arms, long ribbon, reduced sized	$0.50	$2.50

5 Ghirsh, Ah1401-AD1981, KM#84

	Worn	New
10 Ghirsh, AH1403-AD1983, KM#59.4, Copper-Nickel, Denomination/Arms, reduced size	$7.00	$20.00
10 Ghirsh, AH1397-1400-AD1977-80, KM#59.5, Copper-Nickel, Thin denomination and legend/Arms	$0.50	$2.75

	Worn	New
10 Ghirsh, AH1396-98-AD1976-78, KM#67, Copper-Nickel, Denomination/Arms in wheat ears, FAO	$0.30	$1.50
10 Ghirsh, AH1396-AD1976, KM#68, Copper-Nickel, Denomination/Arms long legend above	$0.25	$1.25

50 Ghirsh, AH1396-AD1976, KM#69

	Worn	New
10 Ghirsh, AH1401-AD1981, KM#85, Copper-Nickel, Cow and calf, FAO/Arms	$0.60	$2.50
10 Ghirsh, AH1398-AD1978, KM#95, Copper-Nickel, Clasped hands, Arab Economic Unity/Arms	$0.60	$2.50

	Worn	New
20 Ghirsh, AH1405-AD1985, KM#96, Copper-Nickel, FAO above denomination/Arms		$3.00
20 Ghirsh, AH1403-AD1983, KM#98, Copper-Nickel, Denomination/Arms, long ribbon		$5.00
50 Ghirsh, AH1396-AD1976, KM#69, Copper-Nickel, Denomination, Arab Cooperative/Arms, legend around, dates below	$1.00	$4.50

	Worn	New
50 Ghirsh, AH1397-AD1977, KM#73, Copper-Nickel, 8th Anniversary of 1969 Revolt/Arms, legends above and below	$1.00	$4.50

Pound, AH1398-AD1978, KM#75

| 5 Ghirsh, AH1408-AD1987, KM#100, Aluminum-Bronze, Denomination/Central Bank building | $0.40 | $1.00 |

On May 4, 2004, Staff Sergeant Christopher Rowell assigned to the Parwan Provincial Reconstruction Team hands-out toys to students in Gulbahar, Afghanistan. The Parwan Provincial Reconstruction Team donated toys, clothes, and school supplies on behalf of a church in the United States to the Gulbahar High School and Orphanage in Afghanistan.

US ARMY PHOTO BY SSG VERNELL HALL

	Worn	New
25 Ghirsh, AH1408-AD1987, KM#102.1, Aluminum-Bronze, Denomination partial dashes around/Central Bank building	$0.85	$3.50
25 Ghirsh, AH1408-AD1987, KM#102.2, Aluminum-Bronze, Denominationl dashes around/Central Bank building	$1.00	$4.00
25 Ghirsh, AH1409-AD1989, KM#108, Stainless Steel, Denomination/Central Bank building	$0.50	$2.25
50 Ghirsh, AH1408-AD1987, KM#103, Aluminum-Bronze, Denomination/Central Bank building	$0.75	$3.75

	Worn	New
10 Ghirsh, AH1408-AD1987, KM#107, Aluminum-Bronze, Denomination/Central Bank building	$0.75	$3.00

25 Ghirsh, AH1408-AD1987, KM#102.1

	Worn	New
20 Ghirsh, AH1408-AD1987, KM#101.1, Aluminum-Bronze, Small denomiantion/Central Bank building	$0.60	$2.50
20 Ghirsh, AH1408-AD1987, KM#101.2, Aluminum-Bronze, Large denomiantion/Central Bank building	$0.60	$2.50

Capt Evia Rodriguez of the 478th Battalion shows a local Iraqi girl how to use a toothbrush at Al Uruba grade school in Baghdad.

	Worn	New
Pound, AH1409-AD1989, KM#106, Stainless Steel, Denomination/Central Bank building	$0.75	$3.75
1/4 Dinar, AH1415-AD1994, KM#117, Brass plated steel, Denomination and legends/Central Bank building	Rare	
1/2 Dinar, AH1415-AD1994, KM#118, Brass plated steel, Denomination and legends/Central Bank building	Rare	
Dinar, AH1415-AD1994, KM#112, Brass, Denomination and legends/Central Bank building	$0.35	$1.50

	Worn	New
50 Ghirsh, AH1409-AD1989, KM#105, Aluminum-Bronze, Denomination/map with legend	$0.75	$3.75
50 Ghirsh, AH1409-AD1989, KM#109, Stainless Steel, Denomination/Central Bank building	$0.65	$2.75
Pound, AH1408-AD1987, KM#104, Aluminum-Bronze, Denomination/Central Bank building	$2.00	$7.00

Pound, AH1408-AD1987, KM#104

	Worn	New
2 Dinar, AH1415-AD1994, KM#113, Brass plated steel, Denomination and legends/Central Bank building	$0.75	$3.00
5 Dinars, AH1417-AD1996, KM#114, Brass, Denomination and legends/Central Bank building	$1.00	$4.50
5 Dinars, AH1424-AD2003, KM#119, Brass, Denomination and legends/Central Bank building, reduced to 19mm	$1.00	$4.50
10 Dinars, AH1417-AD1996, KM#115.1, Brass, Denomination and legends/Central Bank building, thin inscription	$1.50	$6.50

	Worn	New
10 Dinars, AH1417-AD1996, KM#115.2, Brass, Denomination and legends/Central Bank building, thick inscription	$1.50	$6.50
10 Dinars, AH1424-AD2003, KM#120.1, Brass, Denomination and legends/Central Bank building, 22mm	$1.50	$6.50
10 Dinars, AH1424-AD2003, KM#120.2, Brass, Denomination and revised legends/Central Bank building, 22mm	$1.50	$6.50
20 Dinars, AH1417-AD1996, KM#116.2, Copper-Nickel, Denomination and legends/Central Bank building, 64 beads in boarder	$1.75	$3.50
20 Dinars, AH1417-AD1996, KM#116.1, Copper-Nickel, Denomination and legends/Central Bank building, 72 beads in boarder	$1.75	$3.50
50 Dinars, AH1423-AD2003, KM#121, Copper-Nickel, Denomination and legends/Central Bank building, 24mm	$2.50	$10.00

Syria

	Worn	New
5 Piastres, AH1391-AD1971, KM#100, Aluminum-Bronze, Arms with stars/ Wheat ear, FAO		$0.25

	Worn	New
25 Piastres, AH1392-AD1972, KM#101, Nickel, Arms/Pillar with flames - Al Ba'ath Party		$0.60

	Worn	New
50 Piastres, AH1392-AD1972, KM#102, Nickel, Arms/Flaming torch - Al Ba'ath Party	$0.50	$2.00

Pound, AH1392-AD1972, KM#103

Sgt. Fernando Perez, a team leader with Co. B, TF 1-21 Inf., plays with an Iraqi child while on a joint dismounted patrol with Iraqi Police officers in the city of Kirkuk, Iraq on Dec. 20.

PHOTO BY: SGT. SEAN KIMMONS

	Worn	New
Pound, AH1392-AD1972, KM#103, Nickel, Arms/Flaming torch above map - Al Ba'ath Party	$0.50	$2.50

	Worn	New
2 1/2 Piastres, AH1393-AD1973, KM#104, Aluminum-Bronze, Arms/ Denomination		$0.25

	Worn	New
10 Piastres, AH1394-AD1974, KM#106, Aluminum-Bronze, Arms/Denomination		$0.30

5 Piastres, AH1394-AD1974, KM#105,
Aluminum-Bronze, Arms/Denomination $0.25

25 Piastres, AH1394-AD1974, KM#107, Nickel,
Arms/Denomination $0.10 $0.50

A soldier with the 205th Military Intelligence Brigade interacts with Iraqi children at a school near Balad, Iraq.

U.S. ARMY PHOTO BY SGT. JACK MORSE

	Worn	New
50 Piastres, AH1394-AD1974, KM#108, Nickel, Arms/Denomination above wheat ears	$0.20	$0.75

	Worn	New
5 Piastres, AH1396-AD1976, KM#110, Aluminum-Bronze, Arms/Dam, FAO		$0.25

	Worn	New
Pound, AH1394-AD1974, KM#109, Nickel, Arms/Denomination	$0.30	$2.00

	Worn	New
10 Piastres, AH1396-AD1976, KM#111, Brass, Arms/Dam, FAO	$0.10	$0.25
25 Piastres, AH1396-AD1976, KM#112, Nickel, Arms/Dam, FAO	$0.10	$0.50

25 Piastres, AH1396-AD1976, KM#112

Maj. Elivira M. Brown, 443rd Civil Affairs Batalion helps to unload school supplies at a school in Taji, Iraq on 08 December 2004 in support of Operation Iraqi Children. "Operation Iraqi Children is a grassroots program that aims to provide concerned Americans with the means to reach out to the Iraqi people and help support our soldiers' attempts to assist them."

	Worn	New
50 Piastres, AH1396-AD1976, KM#113, Nickel, Arms/Dam, FAO		$1.00

Pound, AH1396-AD1976, KM#114, Nickel, Arms/Dam, FAO — $0.50 $2.50

	Worn	New
Pound, AH1398-AD1978, KM#115, Nickel, Legend around Arms/Legend around Bust left	$1.50	$5.00

	Worn	New
5 Piastres, AH1399-AD1979, KM#116, Aluminum-Bronze, Arms with three stars/ Denomination	$0.10	$0.25
10 Piastres, AH1399-AD1979, KM#117, Aluminum-Bronze, Arms with three stars/ Denomination	$0.10	$0.30

	Worn	New
25 Piastres, AH1399-AD1979, KM#118, Copper-Nickel, Arms with three stars/Denomination	$0.10	$0.50

50 Piastres, AH1399-AD1979, KM#119, Copper-Nickel, Arms with three stars/Denomination above wheat ears $0.20 $0.75

	Worn	New
Pound, AH1399-AD1979, KM#120.1, Copper-Nickel, Arms with three stars/Denomination	$0.30	$1.50
Pound, AH1412-AD1991, KM#120.2, Stainless Steel, Arms with three stars/Denomination	$0.30	$1.50
Pound, AH1414-AD1994, KM#121, Stainless Steel, Arms with two stars/Denomination		$1.50
25 Pounds, ND(1995), KM#122, Stainless Steel in Bronze ring, Legend around Arms with two stars/Bust left		$7.00
2 Pounds, AH1416-AD1996, KM#125, Stainless Steel, Arms with two stars/Ancient ruins of theater, denomination below		$1.75

U.S. Marine Staff Sergeant Clarence Freeman of the 1st Marines stationed at Camp Pendelton, Calif, spends some precious final moments with his son before embarking on the USS Boxer (LHD-4) for a six month deployment. The USS Boxer (LHD-4), homeported in San Diego, Calif, will be deploying to the Arabian Gulf in support of Operation Southern Watch.

	Worn	New
5 Pounds, AH1416-AD1996, KM#123, Copper-Nickel, Arms with two stars in pentagon/Palace in pentagon		$2.00

10 Pounds, AH1416-17-AD1996-97, KM#124, Copper-Nickel, Arms with two stars/Ancient ruins denomination below **$2.50**

	Worn	New
10 Pounds, AH1417-AD1997, KM#128, Copper-Nickel, Arms with two stars/Map with flag above		$2.50
25 Pounds, AH1416-AD1996, KM#126, Stainless Steel in Bronze ring, Arms in oranate circle/ Building		$6.00
5 Pounds, AH1424-AD2003, KM#129, Nickel clad steel, Arms in pentagon/Palace in pentagon		$1.00
10 Pounds, AH1424-AD2003, KM#130, Copper-Nickel-Zinc, Arms with two stars/ Ancient ruins, denomiantion below		$2.00
25 Pounds, AH1424-AD2003, KM#131, Copper-Nickel-Zinc, Arms with two stars/Central Bank building		$4.50

	Worn	New
Lira, 1967-1980, KM#889a.2, Stainless steel, Bust left/Denomination and date	$0.10	$0.50

5 Lira, 1974-79, KM#905

	Worn	New
2 1/2 Lira, 1969-80, KM#893.2, Stainless steel, Man hiking/Denomination and date	$0.15	$1.50
5 Lira, 1974-79, KM#905, Stainless steel, Man on horseback/Denomination and date	$0.15	$2.00

U.S. ARMY PHOTO BY CPL JAMES P. JOHNSON

Staff Sgt. Charles Cotton from the 1st BRT, Charlie Troop, 10th Cav. Regt. gives a chicken to little Iraqi boy during a humanitarian relief drop in an area of Sadr City, Iraq on November 08, 2004. The frozen chicken giveaway is part of a larger humanitarian relief effort to make the lives of the people better. The soldiers from the 1st BRT are from the 1st Cav Div in Ft. Hood, Texas and are at Iron Horse Base in support of Operation Iraqi Freedom.

Army CH-47 Chinook helicopters carrying a delegation of U.S. Senators and Congressmen prepare to land at the Afghan Army's training site in Policharki, Afghanistan, Aug. 22, 2003. The American envoys are visiting Afghanistan to discuss a variety of issues with Hamid Karzai, President of Afghanistan.

	Worn	New
50 Kurus, 1979, KM#925, Stainless steel, Farm tractor, FAO/Denomination and date	$0.20	$1.75

	Worn	New
Lira, 1979, KM#926, Stainless steel, Farm tractor, FAO/Denomination and date	$0.50	$2.50

	Worn	New
Kurus, 1979, KM#924, Bronze, Draped female bust left/Plant, FAO	$0.25	$3.00

	Worn	New
10 Kurus, 1980, KM#935, Bronze, Draped female bust left/Wheat, FAO	$0.25	$2.50
50 Kurus, 1980, KM#936, Stainless steel, Draped female bust left/Denomination and date	$0.10	$1.00

| Kurus, 1979, KM#924a, Aluminum, Draped female bust left/Plant, FAO | $0.25 | $3.00 |

50 Kurus, 1980, KM#936

| Lira, 1980, KM#937, Stainless steel, Draped female bust left/Denomination and date | $0.40 | $2.00 |

A soldier from Charlie Co. 3-21 Infantry, 25th Infantry Division hands out papers with information about the upcoming Iraqi elections during a dismounted patrol in Mosul, Iraq on January 21, 2005. 3-21 infantry is in Iraq in support of Operaion Iraqi Freedom.

	Worn	New
2 1/2 Lira, 1979, KM#927, Stainless steel, Draped female bust left/Denomination and date	$1.00	$4.00
5 Lira, 1979, KM#928, Stainless steel, Draped female bust left/Denomination and date	$1.25	$7.00

	Worn	New
150 Lira, 1979, KM#929.1, Silver, Draped female bust left/Denomination and date, reeded edge		$6.50
150 Lira, 1979, KM#929.2, Silver, Draped female bust left/Denomination and date, lettered edge, (proof)		$22.50

5 Lira, 1979, KM#928

US ARMY PHOTO BY SGT. APRIL L. JOHNSON

Sergeant First Class Joseph Forbes, member of Charlie Company, 2nd Battalion 108th Infantry Regiment, a New York National Guard unit, gives a "high-five" to an Iraqi child in the town of Alalaa during a cordon and search on the 24 Aug 04. C Co, 2/108th Inf conducts these operations to find Improvised Explosive Devices (IEDs), identify targets and gather intelligence information. C Co., 2/108th is in Iraq supporting Operation Iraqi Freedom.

U.S. Army Reservist Staff Sgt. James Smith, 257th Transportation Company, Las Vegas, Nev., holds his eight month old son Malik for the first time after returning home from a 13-month deployment to Kuwait and Iraq. Members of the 257th were reunited with their families at Nellis Air Force Base, Nev., March 25, 2004.

	Worn	New
5 Kurus, 1980, KM#934, Bronze, Fish/Plant	$0.25	$2.50

	Worn	New
5 Lira, 1980, KM#939, Stainless steel, Fish/Denomination and date	$1.25	$10.00
500 Lira, 1979, KM#931, Silver, Denomination/Children (proof)		$20.00
10000 Lira, 1979, KM#933, Gold, Denomination/Children (proof)		$325.00

2 1/2 Lira, 1980, KM#938, Stainless steel, Fish/Denomination and date	$0.75	$7.50

	Worn	New		Worn	New

500 Lira, 1980, KM#940.1, Silver, Woman with child/
Denomination and date, reeded edge   **$7.50**

500 Lira, 1980, KM#940.2, Silver, Woman with child/
Denomination and date, lettered edge, (proof)   **$20.00**

Bir Lira, ND(1981), KM#942, Silver, Crescent and
star at mountain top/Bust of Ataturk right   **$22.50**

Bir Lira, ND(1981), KM#942a, Gold, Crescent and
star at mountain top/Bust of Ataturk right   **$265.00**

Yarim Lira, ND(1981), KM#941, Silver, Crescent and
star at mountain top/Bust of Ataturk right   **$12.50**

Yarim Lira, ND(1981), KM#941a, Gold, Crescent and
star at mountain top/Bust of Ataturk right   **$135.00**

Lira, 1981, KM#943, Aluminum, Bust left/
Denomination and date, Crescent opens left   **$0.25**

Lira, 1982, KM#990, Aluminum, Bust left/
Denomination and date, Crescent opens right   **$0.25**

Staff Sgt. Shannon Gartner, 957th Multi-Role Bridge Company from the N. D. National Guard, reunites with his daughter Allison. Gartner had just arrived at the Raymond J. Bohn Armory in Bismarck, N.D. after a one year tour in Iraq for Operation Iraqi Freedom.

	Worn	New

5 Lira, 1981, KM#944, Aluminum, Man on horseback/Denomination and date, Crescent opens left ... $0.35

5 Lira, 1982, KM#949.1, Aluminum, Man on horseback/Denomination and date, Crescent opens right ... $0.35

5 Lira, 1983, KM#949.2, Aluminum, Man on horseback/Large denomination and date ... $0.35

	Worn	New

10 Lira, 1981, KM#945, Aluminum, Man with cigarette/Denomination and date, Crescent opens left ... $0.10 ... $0.75

10 Lira, 1982, KM#950.1, Aluminum, Man with cigarette/Denomination and date, Crescent opens right ... $0.10 ... $0.75

10 Lira, 1983, KM#950.2, Aluminum, Man with cigarette/Large denomination and date ... $0.10 ... $0.60

10 Lira, 1982, KM#950.1

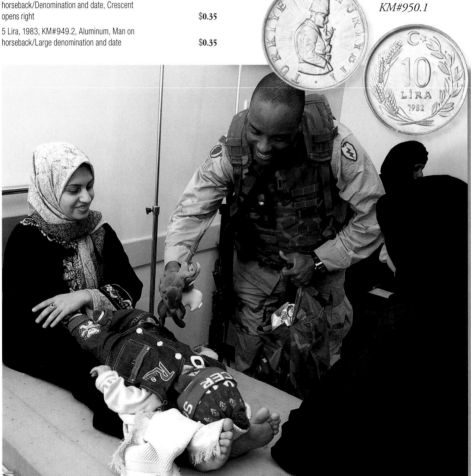

1st Lt. James Harris, a medic platoon leader with TF 1-27 Inf., gives a stuffed animal to an ill child at the Hawija hospital on Dec. 6. Besides toys, Harris and other medics helped donate about $35,000 worth of medical supplies to the hospital.

Capt. Esther Lazo, a physician assistant with Co. C, 225th FSB, checks the breathing pattern of an Iraqi baby during the medical assistance visit at the Al-Taimeem Health Clinic on Dec. 29.

	Worn	New
100 Lira, 1982, KM#951, Copper-Nickel, Soccer player/Date on soccerball-globe	$1.50	$6.00

100 Lira, 1982, KM#951

	Worn	New
20 Lira, 1981, KM#946, Aluminum, Denomination and date/FAO, animals		$3.00

	Worn	New
1500 Lira, 1981, KM#947, Silver, Denomination and date/FAO, animals		$18.50

500 Lira, 1983, KM#957, Copper-Nickel,
Denomination and date/Ancient Lydia coin

Worn	New
	$12.50

1500 Lira, 1983, KM#958, Silver, Denomination
and date/Goat, FAO, (proof) — $40.00

3000 Lira, 1981, KM#948, Silver, Internation
Year of Disabled Persons — $45.00

3000 Lira, ND(1983), KM#960, Silver, Head left in
circle/People encircling Crescent and star (proof)

Worn	New
	$35.00

500 Lira, 1983,
KM#957

2nd Lt. John Herman, a platoon leader with Co. B, TF 1-21 Inf., passes out candy to Iraqi children while on a joint dismounted patrol with Iraqi Police officers Dec. 20 in Kirkuk, Iraq.

PHOTO BY SGT. SEAN KIMMONS

	Worn	New
Lira, 1984, KM#962.1, Aluminum, Bust left/ Large denomination and date		$0.20
Lira, 1985-89, KM#962.2, Aluminum, Bust left/ Small denomination and date		$0.20
5 Lira, 1984-89, KM#963, Aluminum, Bust left/ Denomination and date		$0.50
10 Lira, 1984-89, KM#964, Aluminum, Bust left/ Denomination and date	$0.10	$0.30
20 Lira, 1984-89, KM#965, Copper-Nickel, Bust left/Denomination and date	$0.10	$1.00
25 Lira, 1985-89, KM#975, Aluminum, Bust left/ Denomination and date	$0.10	$0.40
50 Lira, 1984-87, KM#966, Copper-Nickel-Zinc, Bust left/Denomination and date	$0.10	$0.50
50 Lira, 1988-94, KM#987, Aluminum-Bronze, Bust left/Denomination and date		$0.25
100 Lira, 1984-88, KM#967, Copper-Nickel-Zinc, Bust left/Denomination and date	$0.20	$0.85
100 Lira, 1988-94, KM#988, Aluminum-Bronze, Bust left/Denomination and date		$0.20
100 Lira, 1988, KM#988a, Silver, Bust left/ Denomination and date, (proof)		$75.00
500 Lira, ND(1984), KM#968, Copper-Nickel, Denomination and date/Fish, FAO		$25.00

	Worn	New
500 Lira, ND(1986), KM#979, Copper-Nickel, Denomination/FAO, basket, dates, (proof)		$10.00
500 Lira, 1989-97, KM#989, Aluminum-Bronze, Bust left/Denomination and date		$0.60
1000 Lira, 1986, KM#985, Nickel-Bronze, Denomination/Doves (proof)		$12.00
1000 Lira, ND(1987), KM#980, Copper-Nickel, Denomination/Window - Shelter for Homeless (proof)		$10.00

1000 Lira, ND (1987), KM#980

Sgt. Gifari Mahmoud, a forward observer with Co. B, TF 1-21 Inf., claps along with Iraqi children as his joint dismounted patrol passes through their neighborhood Dec. 20 in Kirkuk, Iraq.

PHOTO BY SGT. SEAN KIMMONS

1000 Lira, ND(1988), KM#991, Copper-Nickel,
Denomination/City view with four spires, (proof)

1000 Lira, 1990, KM#996, Copper-Zinc-Nickel,
Denomination and date/Tree within fencing

1000 Lira, 1990-94, KM#997, Copper-Zinc-Nickel,
Bust left/Denomination and date

	Worn	New
1000 Lira, ND(1988)...		$10.00
1000 Lira, 1990...		$8.50
1000 Lira, 1990-94...	$0.15	$2.00

Worn New

1000 Lira, 1995-97, KM#1028, Bronze clad Brass,
Bust left/Denomination and date $1.00

2500 Lira, 1991-97, KM#1015, Nickel-Bronze,
Bust left/ Leaves $0.25 $3.00

5000 Lira, 1991, KM#1005, Copper-Nickel,
Denomination/Archway with banner, (proof) $7.50

	Worn	New
10 Bin Lira, 1998-99, KM#1027.2, Copper-Nickel-Zinc, Bust left/Flower, reeded edge with TC	$0.10	$3.00

	Worn	New
5000 Lira, ND(1992), KM#1018, Copper-Nickel, Denomination/Ship, (proof)		$8.50
5000 Lira, 1992-94, KM#1025, Nickel-Bronze, Bust left/Flowers	$0.25	$3.00
5000 Lira, 1995-99, KM#1029.1, Brass, Bust left/Flowers, reduced size		$0.75
5000 Lira, 1999, KM#1029.2, Brass, Bust left/Flowers, reduced size and weight		$0.75

	Worn	New
10 Bin Lira, 1994, KM#1042, Copper-Nickel-Zinc, Denomination and flower/Olympic rings and rays		$3.75
25 Bin Lira, 1995-2000, KM#1041, Copper-Nickel-Zinc, Bust left/Rose	$0.30	$3.00

	Worn	New
25 Bin Lira, 1995, KM#1043, Copper-Nickel-Zinc, Three heads, wings above/Rose		$5.00
25 Bin Lira, 2001, KM#1104, Copper-Zinc, Bust left/Denomination and date		$2.50
50000 Lira, 1995, KM#1037, Brass, Denomination and date/Sea turtle		$20.00
10 Bin Lira, 1994-97, KM#1027.1, Copper-Nickel-Zinc, Bust left/Flower, reeded edge with TURKIYE	$0.10	$3.00

Local residents sign one of many banners being sent to the troops over seas during a troop support rally in Bellevue hosted by Operation Support Our Troops. The mission of Operation Support Our Troops is to provide a process and forum for Americans of diverse interests, backgrounds and walks of life to come together to demonstrate to members of the Armed Forces and their Commander in Chief that they are supported and deeply appreciated for their service. The goal is to ensure that they know that United We Stand and Divided We Fall are not empty words, but words to which we subscribe. According to Bellevue police, over nine thousand people showed up for a very peaceful rally.

BAGRAM AIR BASE, Afghanistan -- (From left) Staff Sgt. Stephen Manley, Senior Airman Robert Welch, Tech. Sgt. Xavier Sanford and Senior Airman Gary McCormick present the colors during a change of command ceremony. Sergeant Sanford is assigned to the 455th Expeditionary Logistics Readiness Squadron, and Sergeant Manley and Airmen Welch and McCormick are assigned to the 455th Expeditionary Security Forces Squadron.

	Worn	New
50 Bin Lira, ND(1996), KM#1050, Copper-Nickel-Zinc, Globe in wreath/Denomination		$4.50
50 Bin Lira, 1996-2000, KM#1056, Copper-Nickel-Zinc, Bust left/Denomination		$3.50
50000 Lira, 1999, KM#1103, Aluminum, Denomination and date/Man with wine		$0.75

	Worn	New
50 Bin Lira, 2001-02, KM#1105, Copper-Nickel-Zinc, Bust left in circle/Denomination and date		$3.00
100000 Lira, 1999-2000, KM#1078, Copper-Nickel-Zinc,Denomination/Bust right		$3.00
100000 Lira, 1999-2000, KM#1079, Copper-Nickel-Zinc,Denomination/75th Anniversary of Republic		$4.00
100 Bin Lira, 2001-03, KM#1106, Copper-Nickel-Zinc, Bust right in circle/Denomination and date		$3.50
250 Bin Lira, 2002-03, KM#1137, Copper-Nickel-Zinc, Bust facing in circle/Denomination and date		$1.75
400000 Lira, 1996, KM#1051, Bronze, City view/Habitat II logo		$12.50
500000 Lira, 1998, KM#1138, Copper-Nickel, Denomination and date/Bust left		$18.00

	Worn	New
500000 Lira, 1999, KM#1081, Copper-Nickel, Denomination and date/Trojan Horse		$15.00
500000 Lira, 2002, KM#1161, Copper-Nickel, Denomination and date/ Sheep		$2.50
750000 Lira, 1997, KM#1058, Bronze, Denomination and date/Bat winged man in flight		$10.00
750000 Lira, 1997, KM#1059, Bronze, Denomination and date/Stylized bird and tree		$12.50
750000 Lira, 1998, KM#1068, Bronze, Denomination and date/ Wheel of trees		$12.50
750000 Lira, 2002, KM#1162, Copper-Nickel, Denomination and date/Ram		$3.50
1000000 Lira, 2002, KM#1163, Copper-Nickel, Denomination and date/Man in turban facing		$5.00
1000000 Lira, 2002-03, KM#1139, Brass in Copper-Nickel ring, Building and legend/Actual date and legend (Struck by vending machine at the Istanbul Mint with day, month and year)		$15.00
5000000 Lira, 2001, KM#1110, Bronze, Inscription/People		$10.00
5 Kurus, 2005, KM#1165, Copper-Nickel, Bust left in circle/Denomination and date		$0.25

	Worn	New
10 Kurus, 2005, KM#1166, Copper-Nickel, Bust right in circle/Denomination and date		$0.45
25 Kurush, 2005, KM#1167, Copper-Nickel, Bust facing in circle/denomination and date		$1.00
50 Kurush, 2005, KM#1168, Copper-Nickel, Bust right in circle/Denomination and date		$2.00
Kurus, 2005, KM#1164, Brass, Bust left in circle/Denomination and date		$0.15
Lira, 2005, KM#1169, Brass with Copper-Nickel ring, Bust 3/4 left in circle/Denomination and date		$3.50

United Arab Emirates

	Worn	New
Fils, AH1393-1418-AD1973-97, KM#1, Bronze, Legend and denomination/Three palm trees, FAO	$0.20	$0.75

	Worn	New
5 Fils, Ah1393-1409-AD1973-89, KM#2.1, Bronze, Legend and denomination/Fish, FAO, 22mm	$0.10	$0.50

A family member of Electrician's Mate 1st Class Charles Jones, a Sailor aboard the guided missile frigate USS Reuben James (FFG 57), clutches a star with his fathers name inscribed on it shortly after the ship returned to homeport. Family members made a banner with a star for each Reuben James Sailor while the ship was on an extended nine-month deployment in support of Operation Iraqi Freedom.

5 Fils, AH1416-AD1996, KM#2.2, Bronze, Legend and denomination/Fish, FAO, 17mm — Worn $0.10, New $0.50

10 Fils, AH1393-1409-AD1973-89, KM#3.1, Bronze, Legend and denomination/Sailboat, 27mm — Worn $0.25, New $1.00

10 Fils, AH1416-AD1996, KM#3.2, Bronze, Legend and denomination/Sailboat, 19mm — Worn $0.20, New $0.80

25 Fils, AH1393-1419-AD1973-98, KM#4, Copper-Nickel, Legend and denomination/Gazelle — Worn $0.20, New $0.75

50 Fils, AH1393-1409-AD1973-89, KM#5, Copper-Nickel, Legend and denomination/Oil derricks — Worn $0.35, New $1.65

	Worn	New
50 Fils, AH1415-19-AD1995-98, KM#16, Copper-Nickel, Legend and denomination/Oil derricks, seven sided	$0.25	$1.35
Dirham, AH1393-1409-AD1973-89, KM#6.1, Copper-Nickel, Legend and denomination/Jug, 28mm	$0.50	$2.25
Dirham, AH1415-19-AD1995-98, KM#6.2, Copper-Nickel, Legend and denomination/Jug, 23mm	$0.35	$1.85

Dirham, ND(1987), KM#14

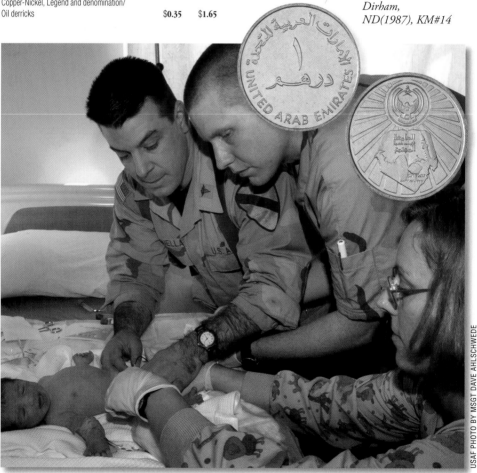

(Front to Back) Lt Wilson, Capt. Vernon and Maj. Spinella tend to Hassin, an Iraqi baby born on election day, Jan. 30 2005. Soldiers of the 86th Combat Support Hospital (CSH) deployed over 500 Soldiers from Fort Campbell to Baghdad, Iraq. The 86th CSH made history by being the first unit in combat to collect platelets from Soldiers using a technique called aphaeresis. Commander Colonel Casper Jones remarked, "Our Eagle Medics are taking care of the wounded and sick regardless of their origins, beliefs, or creed. We are saving life, limb, and eyesight practically every day."

	Worn	New
Dirham, ND(1986), KM#10, Copper-Nickel, Legend and denomination/Olympic rings and chess pieces	$2.00	$9.00
Dirham, ND(1987), KM#11, Copper-Nickel, Legend and denomination/Offshore oil drilling	$2.00	$9.00
Dirham, ND(1987), KM#14, Copper-Nickel, Legend and denomination/Open book with rays	$1.75	$8.00

	Worn	New
Dirham, ND(1990), KM#15, Copper-Nickel, Legend and denomination/Eagle palying soccer	$1.50	$6.50
Dirham, ND(1998), KM#32, Copper-Nickel, Legend and denomination/Dubai National Bank building		$3.50
Dirham, ND(1998), KM#35, Copper-Nickel, Legend and denomination/Bird in window frame		$3.50
Dirham, ND(1998), KM#38, Copper-Nickel, Legend and denomination/Circular logo		$3.50

A U.S. soldier sends a "message to Mom" from Camp Virginia, Kuwait, Dec. 13, 2004, during a USO show hosted by Gen. Richard B. Myers, Chairman of the Joint Chiefs of Staff.

	Worn	New
Dirham, ND(1998), KM#39, Copper-Nickel, Legend and denomination/Flame		$3.50
Dirham, ND(1999), KM#40, Copper-Nickel, Legend and denomination/Ocean oil well		$3.50
Dirham, AH1420 (1999), KM#41, Copper-Nickel, Legend and denomination/Square design		$3.50

50 Dirhams, AH1410 (1990), KM#17

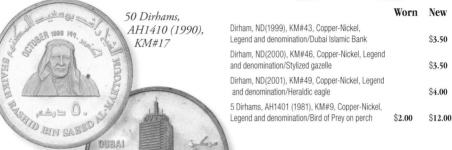

	Worn	New
Dirham, ND(1999), KM#43, Copper-Nickel, Legend and denomination/Dubai Islamic Bank		$3.50
Dirham, ND(2000), KM#46, Copper-Nickel, Legend and denomination/Stylized gazelle		$3.50
Dirham, ND(2001), KM#49, Copper-Nickel, Legend and denomination/Heraldic eagle		$4.00
5 Dirhams, AH1401 (1981), KM#9, Copper-Nickel, Legend and denomination/Bird of Prey on perch	$2.00	$12.00

Members of the North Carolina National Guards' 210th Military Police Company, returned home to Asheville N.C. where thier families have been waiting for them for over 15 months while the 210th was serving in Iraq.

US AIR FORCE PHOTO BY SRA FRANCISCO V. GOVEA II

	Worn	New
25 Dirhams, ND(1998), KM#33, Silver, Legend and denomination/Dubai National Bank building		$35.00
25 Dirhams, ND(2000), KM#44, Silver, Legend and denomination/Dubai Islamic Bank, (proof)		$35.00
50 Dirhams, AH1400 (1980), KM#7, Silver, Legend and denomination/Children dancing, (proof)		$21.50
50 Dirhams, AH1410 (1990), KM#17, Silver, Shaikh Rashid Bin Saeed Al-Maktoum/Dubai International Trade Center, (proof)		$70.00

Yemen Arab Republic

	Worn	New
Fils, AH1394-AD1974, KM#Y33, Aluminum, Denomination and date/Arms	$3.00	$10.00

	Worn	New
Fils, AH1394-1400-AD1974-80, KM#Y33, Aluminum, Denomination and date/Arms, (proof)		$1.50

	Worn	New
5 Fils, AH1394-1400-AD1974-80, KM#Y34, Brass, Denomination and date/Arms	$0.50	$2.50

	Worn	New
10 Fils, AH1394-AD1400, KM#Y35, Brass, Denomination and date/Arms	$0.50	$2.50
25 Fils, AH1394-1400-AD1974-80, KM#Y36, Copper-Nickel, Denomination and date/Arms	$0.25	$2.50
50 Fils, AH1394-1405-AD1974-85, KM#Y37, Copper-Nickel, Denomination and date/Arms	$0.35	$2.50

	Worn	New
Riyal, AH1396-1405-AD1976-85, KM#Y42, Copper-Nickel, Denomination and date/Arms	$0.50	$2.50
Fils, AH1398-AD1978, KM#Y43, Aluminum, Legend above Arms/Denomination and date		$3.00
5 Fils, AH1394-AD1974, KM#Y38, Brass, Legend above Arms/Denomination and date		$0.25

	Worn	New
10 Fils, AH1394-AD1974, KM#Y39, Brass, Legend above Arms/Denomination and date		$0.25

	Worn	New
25 Fils, AH1394-AD1974, KM#Y40, Copper-Nickel, Legend above Arms/Denomination and date	$0.20	$1.00

	Worn	New
50 Fils, AH1394-AD1974, KM#Y41, Copper-Nickel, Legend above Arms/Denomination and date	$0.25	$1.25
Riyal, AH1398-AD1978, KM#Y44, Copper-Nickel, Legend above Arms/Denomination and date		$5.00
2 1/2 Riyals, AH1395-AD1975, KM#14, Silver, Arms, date and denomination/Oil field		$15.00
5 Riyals, AH1395-AD1975, KM#15, Silver, Arms, date and denomination/Mona Lisa		$20.00
25 Riyals, AH1401-AD1981, KM#Y46, Silver, Arms and date/Bust right, International Year of the Disabled Person		$32.50
25 Riyals, AH1403-AD1983, KM#Y45, Silver, Arms in wreath/Children dancing, (proof)		$18.50
25 Riyals, AH1405-AD1985, KM#Y49, Silver, Arms in wreath/Three women, (proof)		$42.50

Yemen Democratic Republic

	Worn	New
5 Fils, AH1393-1404-AD1973-84, KM#4, Aluminum, Denomination and date/Lobster	$0.15	$0.75
25 Fils, 1976-84, KM#5, Copper-Nickel, Star design/Sailboat	$0.25	$1.50
50 Fils, 1976-84, KM#6, Copper-Nickel, Star design/Sailboat	$0.35	$2.50
10 Fils, 1981, KM#9, Aluminum, Legend above building/Denomination	$0.35	$2.00
100 Fils, 1981, KM#10, Copper-Nickel, Legend above building/Denomination	$0.50	$3.00
250 Fils, 1981, KM#11, Copper-Nickel, Legend above building/Denomination	$1.50	$5.50

Yemen Republic (Unified)

Riyal, AH1414-AD1993, KM#25, Stainless steel, Legend, denomination and date/Arms	$1.25
5 Riyals, AH1414-21-AD1993-2001, KM#26, Stainless steel, Legend, denomination and date/Building	$1.75
10 Riyals, AH1416-24-AD1995-2003, KM#27, Stainless steel, Legend, denomination and date/Bridge	$2.75

PAPER MONEY

The mulberry pulp paper note was first introduced in China in the 1300s and general use of paper money had gained wide acceptance in European by the mid 1600s. Merchants favored paper note exchanges to the transfer of large sums of gold or silver coinage over greater distances. Representative paper money was an attractive option because it established a higher level of security for the conduct of commerce and trade.

In the Middle East the use of paper documents as negotiable instruments began sometime in the 12th or 13th century, though dependence on silver coinage remained at the heart of most regional economies until the 19th century. Circulating bank notes appeared in the region through European influences mainly during the mid to late 19th century.

General Gordon issued emergency paper money during the Siege of Khartoum in 1884, in denominations of 1 to 5000 piastres. On a broader scale the Ottoman Empire began to introduce paper money into the region in the 1840's. By the turn of the century paper money was being used for daily commerce throughout the Middle East.

Today, most bank notes are issued by a nation's central bank. Modern paper money employs many security features that have been in use for centuries, as well as some that are new to the 21st century. Intaglio printing, which employs refined engraving, creates handsome portraits and intricate designs that are difficult to copy. Additional anti-counterfeiting devices such as watermarked papers and embedded metallic threads are popular. Foil applications, metallic or color shifting inks, as well as distinctive serial numbering systems all add to a bank notes security and acceptance. Security is the major issue, as most modern currency is not backed by gold or silver bullion reserves, but by supplies of other major currencies,

Iraq 10 Dinars #81

Sgt. Maj. Ichina, Sgt5. Maj. of 103rd Armored Battalion, Task Force Dragoon, 28th Infantry Division out of Penn., gives candy to local children while visiting a polling station in a village on the outskirts of Bayji, Iraq.

such as the Euro or U.S. Dollar, and faith in a government's ability to control their economy.

The use of ascending sizes for the increase in denominations in a series and major color for particular denominations appears obvious when complete sets of issued types are viewed together. Often the major color remains the same in successive series over time, so as to ease the transition of old to new designs for the public.

The paper money of a nation is a wonderful propaganda tool to instill its history, its politics, and its national pride on something that most people use every day. National patriotism, acceptances of a governing body, religious or political beliefs are all agendas, which can be and often are advanced through bank note themes and images.

In times of conflict and war, banknotes can often become a pivotal point of marginal advantage. Invading armies sometimes produce counterfeit banknotes to flood the market and upset their adversary's economic

stability. Propaganda leaflets often adopt the style of circulating banknotes to demean and degrade the strength of a countries currency. One will notice that the notes of Iraq during the later years of the Saddam regime were printed using the offset method, with few security features. This made the series very vulnerable to attack through counterfeiting and propaganda.

The listings in this section are arranged by country and by series within country. The series are arranged in ascending fashion simply by first date of issue. Values are given for **worn** or circulated and **new** or uncirculated notes. A note, which has circulated, will show signs of actual use and handling. The corners may be rounded, the edges may have small tears, there might be folds or tiny pinholes and sometimes even writing on the note. An uncirculated note will appear to be new as when it was issued. It will be crisp to the touch and have sharp corners and edges, with none of the wear features evident on circulated notes.

Afghanistan 10 Afghanis #55

Djibouti 5000 Francs #43

	Worn	New
Afghanistan		
Da Afghanistan Bank		
1979 Issue		
10 Afghanis, #55, Arms / Mountain road	$0.20	$0.60
20 Afghanis, #56, Arms / Building and mountains	$0.25	$1.00
50 Afghanis, #57, Arms / Dar-al-Aman Palace in Kabul	$0.25	$1.00
100 Afghanis, #58, Arms & farm worker / Hydroelectric dam	$0.50	$2.00
500 Afghanis, #59, Bank arms & horsemen / Fortress at Kabul	$2.00	$12.50
500 Afghanis, #60, Bank arms & horsemen Fortress in Kabul	$1.00	$2.00
1000 Afghanis, #61, Bank arms, horseman & Mosque / Victory Arch	$2.50	$5.00
1993 Issue		
5000 Afghanis, #62, Bank arms of horseman and Mosque / Tomb of King Habibullah	$0.50	$2.00
10,000 Afghanis, #63, Bank arms of horseman & Gateway / Arched gateway at Bost	$0.75	$3.00

	Worn	New
2002 Issue		
1 Afghanis, #64, Bank seal / Mosque at Mazar-I Sharif	$0.25	$0.50
2 Afghanis, #65, Bank seal / Victory Arch	$0.25	$0.50
5 Afghanis, #66, Bank seal / Fortress at Kabul	$0.25	$0.75
10 Afghanis, #67, Mosque / Victory Arch	$0.50	$1.25
20 Afghanis, #68, Tomb of Arg-e Shahi / King's Palace	$0.50	$1.50
50 Afghanis, #69, Mosque / Salang Pass	$0.50	$3.00
100 Afghanis, #70, Arch at Qila'-e Bost	$2.50	$6.00
500 Afghanis, #71, Airport tower	$12.50	$25.00
1000 Afghanis, #72, Mosque / Tomb of King Habibullah	$25.00	$50.00
Djibouti		
Republique de Djibouti		
Banque Nationale		
1979 Issue		
500 Francs, #36, Male head & rock in sea / Stern of ship	$6.00	$15.00

Afghanistan 100 Afghanis #58

Afghanistan 50 Afghanis #69

Afghanistan 1000 Afghanis #72

Egyptian 1 Pound #50

Egyptian 100 Pounds #53

Sgt. Carlos Gonales from the 13th COSCOM, Logistics Support Area (LAS) Anaconda, Iraq, shows the proper wear of a Kevlar helmet, during a visit to the school in the town of Al Rafae to deliver donated school supplies. Students from Pepperdine University in California donated the supplies.

	Worn	New
1000 Francs, #37, Female head & train / Trader with camels	$10.00	$30.00
5000 Francs, #38, Male head & forest / Aerial view	$35.00	$75.00
10,000 Francs, #39, Woman holding baby / Fish and harbor	$75.00	$150.00

Banque Nationale de Djibouti
1997 Issue

	Worn	New
2000 Francs, #40, Young girl & camel caravan / Statue & Government	$15.00	$30.00
10,000 Francs, #42, President Hassan Gouled Aptidon / Central Bank	$60.00	$125.00

Banque Centrale de Djibouti
2002 Issue

	Worn	New
5000 Francs, #43, Central Bank building & M. Harbi / Three females dancing	$30.00	$55.00

Egypt

Central Bank of Egypt
1978-79 Issue

	Worn	New
25 Piastres, #49, Al-Sayida Aisha Mosque / Stylized A.R.E. Arms	$0.50	$2.00

	Worn	New
1 Pound, #50, Sultan Qait Bay Mosque / Archais statues	$0.50	$1.50
10 Pounds, #51, Al-Rifai Mosque / Pharaoh	$2.00	$10.00
20 Pounds, #52, Muhammed Ali Mosque / Archaic sculptures from Chapel of Sesostris	$5.00	$20.00
100 Pounds, #53, Al-Sayida Zainab Mosque / Pharaoh's mask	$40.00	$100.00

1980-81 Issue

	Worn	New
25 Piastres, #54, Al-Sayida Aisha Mosque / Stylized A.R.E. Arms	$0.30	$1.50
50 Piastres, #55, Al-Azhar Mosque / Ramses II	$0.50	$2.00
5 Pounds, #56, Ibn Toulon Mosque / Bounty of the Nile	$3.00	$15.00

1985 Issue

	Worn	New
25 Piastres, #57, Al-Sayida Aisha Mosque / Stylized A.R.E. Arms	$0.25	$1.00
50 Piastres, #58, Al-Azhar Mosque / Ramses II	$0.25	$1.50

1989-94 Issue

	Worn	New
5 Pounds, #59, Ibn Toulon Mosque / Bounty of the Nile	$1.00	$5.00

Egyptian 50 Piastres #55

Egyptian 5 Pounds #59

Egyptian 50 Pounds #60

Egyptian 5 Pounds #63

	Worn	New
50 Pounds, #60, Abu Hariba Mosque / Isis & Edfu temple	$10.00	$30.00
100 Pounds, #61, Sultan Hassan Mosque / Sphinx	$30.00	$60.00

1995 Issue

	Worn	New
50 Piastres, #62, Al-Azhar Mosque / Ramses II	$0.20	$0.75

2000-03 Issue

	Worn	New
5 Pounds, #63, Mosque of Ahmad ibn Tulun / Ramses II	$1.00	$5.00
10 Pounds, #64, Mosque at center. Carving on back.	$2.00	$8.00
20 Pounds, #65, Muhammed Ali Mosque / Archaic sculptures from Chapel of Sesostris	$5.00	$15.00
50 Pounds, #66, Abu Hariba Mosque / Isis & Edfu temple	$10.00	$27.50
100 Pounds, #67, Sultan Hassan Mosque / Sphinx	$25.00	$50.00

Arab Republic of Egypt
Currency Notes
1971 Issue

	Worn	New
5 Piastres, #180, Queen Nefertiti	$0.25	$3.00
10 Piastres, #181, Militants	$0.25	$4.00

1997-98 Issue

	Worn	New
5 Piastres, #182, Queen Nefertiti	$0.25	$1.25
10 Piastres, #183, Sphinx and pyramids	$0.50	$1.50

1998-99 Issue

	Worn	New
5 Piastres, #184, Queen Nefertiti	$0.25	$1.25
10 Piastres, #185, Sphinx and pyramids	$0.25	$1.00

Ethiopia

National Bank of Ethiopia
1976 Issue

	Worn	New
1 Birr, #30, Youth and longhorns / Waterfall	$2.00	$5.00
5 Birr, #31, Man picking coffee beans / Kudu, caracal and Semien Mountains	$3.25	$9.00
10 Birr, #32, Woman weaving basket / Tractor	$6.00	$15.00
50 Birr, #33, Science students / Fasilides Castle at Gondar	$25.00	$60.00
100 Birr, #34, Warrior / Young man with microscope	$35.00	$90.00

1987 Issue

	Worn	New
1 Birr, #36, Youth and longhorns / Waterfall	$1.00	$2.50
5 Birr, #37, Man picking coffee beans / Kudu, caracal and Semien Mountains	$2.50	$6.00
10 Birr, #38, Woman weaving basket / Tractor	$3.50	$10.00

Egyptian 20 Pounds #65

Egyptian 100 Pounds #67

Ethiopian 5 Birr #47

Ethiopian 10 Birr #48

Ethiopian 50 Birr #49

	Worn	New
50 Birr, #39, Science students / Fasilides Castle at Gondar	$17.50	$40.00
100 Birr, #40, Warrior / Young man with microscope	$35.00	$70.00

1991 Issue

	Worn	New
1 Birr, #41, Youth and longhorns / Waterfall	$0.75	$1.50
5 Birr, #42, Man picking coffee beans / Kudu, caracal and Semien Mountains	$2.00	$4.50
10 Birr, #43, Woman weaving basket / Tractor	$3.75	$7.50
50 Birr, #44, Science students / Fasilides Castle at Gondar	$20.00	$40.00
100 Birr, #45, Warrior / Young man with microscope	$25.00	$50.00

1997 Issue

	Worn	New
1 Birr, #46, Youth and longhorns / Waterfall	$0.25	$0.75
5 Birr, #47, Man picking coffee beans / Kudu, caracal and Semien Mountains	$0.50	$3.00
10 Birr, #48, Woman weaving basket / Tractor	$1.00	$4.00

	Worn	New
50 Birr, #49, Farmer Plowing w/Oxen / Fasilides Castle at Gondar	$3.00	$12.50
100 Birr, #50, Warrior / Young man with microscope	$10.00	$25.00

2003 Issue

	Worn	New
50 Birr, #51, Science students / Fasilides Castle at Gondar	$3.00	$12.50
100 Birr, #52, Warrior / Young man with microscope	$10.00	$25.00

Iran

Bank Markazi Iran

1981 Issue

	Worn	New
200 Rials, #127, Iman Reza Mosque / Tomb of Ibn-e-Sina	$2.00	$6.00
200 Rials, #127A, Imam Reza Mosque / Victory monument	$2,500.00	$6,000.00
500 Rials, #128, Imam Reza Mosque / Winged horses	$4.50	$11.00

Iranian 200 Rials #127

Iranian 100 Rials #132

Iranian 1,000 Rials #129

Iranian 10,000 Rials #131

	Worn	New		Worn	New
1000 Rials, #129, Imam Reza Mosque / Tomb of Hafez	$8.00	$22.50	1000 Rials, #138, Feyzieh Madressa Seminary / Mosque of Omar	$2.50	$5.00
5000 Rials, #130, Imam Reza Mosque / Oil refinery at Tehran	$25.00	$60.00	1000 Rials, #138A, Feyzieh Madressa Seminary / Mosque of Omar	$0.75	$3.00
10,000 Rials, #131, Imam Reza Mosque / National Council of Ministries in Tehran	$30.00	$80.00	5000 Rials, #139, Mullahs leading marchers / Hazrat Masoumeh Shrine	$17.50	$45.00

1981 Second Issue

Central Bank of the Islamic Republic of Iran

	Worn	New		Worn	New
100 Rials, #132, Imam Reza Mosque / Madressa Chahr-Bagh in Isfahan	$0.75	$2.50	**1985-86 Issue**		
5000 Rials, #133, Mullahs leading marchers / Hazrat Masoumeh Shrine	$15.00	$50.00	100 Rials, #140, Ayatollah Moddaress / Parliament	$0.50	$2.00
10,000 Rials, #134, Mullahs leading marchers / Imam Reza Mosque	$15.00	$75.00	2000 Rials, #141, Revolutionists / Kaaba in Mecca	$2.00	$4.00

1982-83 Issue

1992-93 Issue

	Worn	New		Worn	New
100 Rials, #135, Imam Reza Mosque / National Council of Ministries in Teheran	$1.00	$1.75	500 Rials, #142, Khomeini at right / Mosque of Omar	$2.50	$4.00
200 Rials, #136, Mosque / Farmers and tractor	$1.50	$4.50	5000 Rials, #145, Khomeini / Flowers and bird	$3.50	$7.50
500 Rials, #137, Feyzieh Madressa Seminary / Tehran University	$1.00	$2.50	10,000 Rials, #146, Khomeini at right / Mount Damavand	$5.00	$12.50
500 Rials, #137A, Feyzieh Madressa Seminary / Tehran University	$0.75	$1.50	20,000 Rials, #147, Khomeini / large portrait	$5.00	$15.00
			20,000 Rials, #148, Khomeini / small dark portrait	$5.00	$10.00

Iranian 5000 Rials #133

Iranian 200 Rials #136

Iranian 5000 Rials #139

Iraqi 1/4 Dinar #67

Iraqi 25 Dinars #72

Master Sergeant White assigned to the Parwan Provincial Reconstruction Team handout supplies to students in Gulbahar, Afghanistan. The Parwan Provincial Reconstruction Team donated toys, clothes, and school supplies on behalf of a church in the United States to the Gulbahar High School and Orphanage in Afghanistan.

Iraq

Central Bank of Iraq

1976-86 Issue

	Worn	New
1/4 Dinar, #67, Palm trees / Building	$0.30	$1.00
1/2 Dinar, #68, Astrolabe / Minaret of the Great Mosque at Samarra	$0.20	$0.75
1 Dinar, #69, Coin / Musansiriyah School in Baghdad	$0.20	$0.75
5 Dinars, #70, Gali-Ali Beg waterfall / Al-Ukhether Castle	$1.00	$3.00
10 Dinars, #71, Al-Hassan ibn al-Haitham / Hadba minaret in Mosul	$1.00	$3.00
25 Dinars, #72, Three Arabian horses / Abbasid Palace	$0.75	$1.25
25 Dinars, #73, Saddam Hussein & Charging horsemen / Martyr's Monument	$0.75	$2.50

1990 Emergency Gulf War Issue

	Worn	New
25 Dinars, #74, Three Arabian horses / Abbasid Palace	$0.10	$0.50
50 Dinars, #75, Saddam Hussein / Minaret of the Great Mosque at Samarra	$0.10	$0.75

	Worn	New
100 Dinars, #76, Saddam Hussein / Victory Arch Monument	$15.00	$40.00

1992-93 Emergency Issue

	Worn	New
1/4 Dinar, #77, Palm trees / Building	$0.10	$0.40
1/2 Dinar, #78, Astrolabe / Minaret of the Great Mosque at Samarra	$0.10	$0.40
1 Dinar, #79, Coin / Musansiriyah School in Baghdad	$0.10	$0.40
5 Dinars, #80, Saddam Hussein & Temple / Tomb of the unknown soldier	$0.10	$0.40
10 Dinars, #81, Saddam Hussein & Temple / Winged lion statue in Khorsabad	$0.10	$1.50

1994-95 Issue

	Worn	New
50 Dinars, #83, Saddam Hussein / Modern Saddam Bridge	$0.10	$1.50
100 Dinars, #84, Saddam Hussein / Baghdad clock	$0.10	$1.00
250 Dinars, #85, Saddam Hussein / Friese from Liberty monument	$0.10	$1.25

2001-02 Issue

	Worn	New
25 Dinars, #86, Saddam Hussein / Babylon gate on back.	$0.10	$0.75

Iraqi 50 Dinars #75

Iraqi 5 Dinars #80

Iraqi 250 Dinars #85

Iraqi 100 Dinars #87

	Worn	New
100 Dinars, #87, Saddam Hussein / Shenashils of old Baghdad	$0.10	$1.50
250 Dinars, #88, Saddam Hussein / Dome of the Rock	$0.10	$1.50
10,000 Dinars, #89, Saddam Hussein / Al-Musansiriyah University	$1.50	$7.50

2003 Issue

	Worn	New
50 Dinars, #90, Grain silo at Basrah / Date palms	$0.10	$0.50
250 Dinars, #91, Astrolobe at right / Spiral Minaret in Samarra	$0.25	$1.00
500 Dinars, #92, Dockdan Dam / Winged bull statue	$0.50	$1.75
1000 Dinars, #93, Medieval dinar coin / Al-Musansiriyah University	$0.75	$2.50
5000 Dinars, #94, Gali Ali Beg and waterfall / Al-Ukhether fortress	$2.50	$10.00
10,000 Dinars, #95, Abu Ali Hasan Ibn al-Haitham/Hadba Minaret at the Great Nur ad-Din Mosque in Mosul	$5.00	$15.00

	Worn	New
25,000 Dinars, #96, Kurdish farmer / Ancient Babylonian King Hammurabi	$15.00	$27.50

Israel

Bank of Israel
1978-84 Issue

	Worn	New
1 Sheqel, #43, Moses Montefiore / Jaffa Gate	$0.50	$2.00
5 Sheqalim, #44, Chaim Weizmann / Sichem Gate	$0.75	$3.00
10 Sheqalim, #45, Theodor Herzl / Zion Gate	$1.50	$5.00
50 Sheqalim, #46, David Ben-Gurion / Golden Gate	$0.50	$2.00
100 Sheqalim, #47, Ze'ev Jabotinsky / Herod's Gate	$1.50	$6.00
500 Sheqalim, #48, Baron Edmond de Rothschild / Vine leaves	$1.50	$9.00
1000 Sheqalim, #49, Rabbi Moses Maimonides / View of Tiberias	$7.50	$30.00
5000 Sheqalim, #50, Levi Eshkol / Water pipe	$7.50	$45.00
10,000 Sheqalim, #51, Golda Meir / Gathering in front of Moscow synagogue	$10.00	$35.00

Iraqi 50 Dinars #90

Iraqi 1000 Dinars, #93

Iraqi 5000 Dinars #94

Iraqi 25,000 Dinars #96

Israeli 20 New Sheqalim #59

A U.S. Army OH-58D Kiowa Scout on patrol.

PHOTO BY STAFF SGT AARON ALLMON II

	Worn	New
1985-92 Issue		
1 New Sheqel, #51A, Rabbi Moses Maimonides / View of Tiberias	$0.50	$2.00
5 New Sheqalim, #52, Levi Eshkol / Water pipe	$2.50	$20.00
10 New Sheqalim, #53, Golda Meir / Gathering in front of Moscow synagogue	$2.00	$12.50
20 New Sheqalim, #54, Moshe Sharett / Herzlya High School	$10.00	$20.00
50 New Sheqalim, #55, Shmuel Yosef Agnon / Buildings	$25.00	$50.00
100 New Sheqalim, #56, Itzhak Ben-Zvi / Stylized village of Peki'n	$35.00	$75.00
200 New Sheqalim, #57, Zalman Shazar / Schoolgirl writing	$60.00	$120.00
1998 Commemorative		
50 New Sheqalim, #58, Shmuel Yousef Agnon	$25.00	$50.00
1998 Issue		
20 New Sheqalim, #59, Moshe Sharett / Scenes of his life	$7.50	$20.00
50 New Sheqalim, #60, Shmuel Yosef Agnon / Manuscript, pen and glasses	$15.00	$30.00

	Worn	New
100 New Sheqalim, #61, Itzhak Ben-Zvi / Scenes of his life	$25.00	$50.00
200 New Sheqalim, #62, Zalman Shazar / Scenes of his life	$50.00	$100.00

Jordan

Central Bank of Jordan
1975-92 Issue

	Worn	New
1/2 Dinar, #17, King Hussein / Jerash	$1.50	$5.00
1 Dinar, #18, King Hussein / Al-Aqsa Mosque	$2.50	$7.50
5 Dinars, #19, King Hussein / Al-Hazne, Petra	$12.50	$25.00
10 Dinars, #20, King Hussein / Cultural palace and Roman amphitheater	$20.00	$40.00
20 Dinars, #21, King Hussein / Electrical power station at Zerga	$35.00	$80.00

1992-93 Issue

	Worn	New
1/2 Dinar, #32, King Hussein / Qusayr Amra fortress	$2.00	$4.00
1 Dinar, #24, King Hussein / Ruins of Jerash	$3.00	$6.00
5 Dinars, #25, King Hussein / Treasury of Petra	$12.50	$25.00
10 Dinars, #26, King Hussein / Al-Rabadh Castle	$25.00	$50.00
20 Dinars, #27, King Hussein / Al-Aqsa Mosque	$45.00	$95.00

Jordan 1/2 Dinar #17

Jordan 10 Dinars #20

Jordan 5 Dinars #25

Jordan 20 Dinars #27

	Worn	New
1995-2002 Issue		
1/2 Dinar, #28, King Hussein / Qusayr Amra fortress	$1.50	$3.00
1 Dinar, #29, King Hussein / Ruins of Jerash	$2.50	$5.00
5 Dinars, #30, King Hussein / Treasury of Petra	$8.50	$17.50
10 Dinars, #31, King Hussein / Al-Rabadh Castle	$17.50	$35.00
20 Dinars, #32, King Hussein / Al-Aqsa Mosque	$30.00	$50.00
50 Dinars, #33, King Abdullah II / Raghadan Palace	$60.00	$125.00
2002 Issue		
1 Dinar, #34, Sherif Hussein Ibn Ali / Great Arab Revolt	$1.50	$3.00
5 Dinars, #35, King Abdullah I / Ma'an Palace	$6.00	$12.50
10 Dinars, #36, King Talal ibn Abdullah / Camels at Petra	$15.00	$30.00
20 Dinars, #37, King Hussein / Al-Aqsa Mosque	$25.00	$50.00
50 Dinars, #38, King Abdullah II / 1Raghadan Palace	$55.00	$110.00

Kuwait

	Worn	New
Central Bank of Kuwait **1980-91 Issue**		
1/4 Dinar, #11, Arms / Oil refinery	$2.00	$6.00
1/2 Dinar, #12, Arms / Harbor scene	$3.00	$7.50
1 Dinar, #13, Arms / Old city fortress	$4.00	$10.00
5 Dinars, #14, Arms / Seif Palace	$8.00	$30.00
10 Dinars, #15, Arms / Large dhow	$10.00	$32.50
20 Dinars, #16, Arms / Justice Center on Kuwait	$12.50	$32.50
1992 Issue		
1/4 Dinar, #17, Arms / Oil refinery	$1.00	$4.00
1/2 Dinar, #18, Arms / Harbor scene	$3.50	$7.00
1 Dinar, #19, Arms / Old city fortress	$4.50	$9.00
5 Dinars, #20, Arms / Seif Palace	$20.00	$45.00
10 Dinars, #21, Arms / Large dhow	$30.00	$75.00
20 Dinars, #22, Arms / Justice Center on Kuwait	$50.00	$125.00
1993 Commemorative		
1 Dinar, not legal tender, #CS1, Second Anniversary of Liberation - Burning oilfields		$20.00

Jordan 10 Dinars #31

Jordan 50 Dinars #38

*Kuwaiti Commemorative 1
Dinar #CS1*

Kuwaiti 20 Dinars #22

Kuwaiti 1 Dinar #25

Sgt. Anthony Gains from Logistics Support Area (LSA) Anaconda, hands out backpacks to children at a school in the town of Al Rafae, Iraq. Students from Pepperdine University in California donated the supplies.

	Worn	New
1994 Issue		
1/4 Dinar, #23, Arms / Girls playing game	$1.00	$3.00
1/2 Dinar, #24, Arms / Boys playing game	$2.00	$6.00
1 Dinar, #25, Arms / Aerial view of harbor	$4.00	$10.00
5 Dinars, #26, Arms / Oil refinery	$20.00	$40.00
10 Dinars, #27, Arms / Pearl fisherman and dhow	$35.00	$75.00
20 Dinars, #28, Arms / Central bank at bottom	$50.00	$110.00

2001 Commemorative Issue

	Worn	New
1 Dinar, not legal tender, #CS2, Tenth Anniversary of Liberation - Soldier raising flag		$17.50

Lebanon

Banque du Liban

1978 Issue

	Worn	New
1 Livre, #61, Columns of Baalbek / Jeita Cavern	$1.00	$3.00
5 Livre, #62, Buildings / Bridge over Kalb river	$0.50	$3.00
10 Livre, #63, Ruins of Anjar / Large sea rocks.	$0.50	$2.00
25 Livre, #64, Crusader Castle at Saida / Ruin on rock outcroping	$0.50	$2.00
50 Livre, #65, Ruins of temple of Bacchus at Baalbek / Building complex	$0.50	$2.50
100 Livre, #66, Palais Beit-ed-din / Snowy cedars	$0.50	$2.50
250 Livre, #67, Ruins at Tyras on both sides	$1.50	$4.00

1993 Issue

	Worn	New
500 Livres, #68, Beirut city view / Ruins	$1.00	$3.00
1000 Livres, #69, Map / Ruins and modern building	$1.00	$2.50
10,000 Livres, #70, Ancient ruins at Tyros / City ruins	$7.50	$20.00
5000 Livres, #71, Geometric patterns	$5.00	$10.00
20,000 Livres, #72, Geometric patterns	$17.50	$35.00
50,000 Livres, #73, Geometric patterns	$40.00	$80.00
100,000 Livres, #74, Geometric patterns	$50.00	$110.00

1998-99 Issue

	Worn	New
5000 Livres, #75, Geometric patterns: Squares	$3.50	$7.00
10,000 Livres, #76, Geometric patterns: Figures standing on rock outcroping	$8.50	$17.50
50,000 Livres, #77, Geometric patterns: Boat, diamond	$35.00	$70.00

Kuwaiti 5 Dinars #26

Kuwaiti 10 Dinars #27

Lebanon 10 Livre #63

Lebanon 500 Livres #68

	Worn	New
100,000 Livres, #78, Geometric patterns: Grapes and grain	$50.00	$100.00

2001 Issue

	Worn	New
5000 Livres, #79, Geometric patterns: Squares	$3.00	$6.00
20,000 Livres, #80, Geometric patterns	$17.50	$35.00
50,000 Livres, #81, Geometric patterns: Boat & diamond	$35.00	$70.00
100,000 Livres, #82, Geometric patterns: Grapes and grain	$50.00	$100.00

Oman

Central Bank of Oman

1977-85 Issue

	Worn	New
100 Baisa, #13, Arms / Port of Qaboos	$2.00	$3.00
200 Baisa, #14, Arms / Rustaq Fortress	$2.00	$3.50
1/4 Rial, #15, Arms / Jalali Fortress	$2.50	$5.00
1/2 Rial, #16, Arms / Sumail Fortress	$4.00	$8.00
1 Rial, #17, Arms/ Rustaq Fortress	$8.00	$16.00
5 Rials, #18, Arms / Jalali Fortress	$25.00	$40.00
10 Rials, #19, Arms / Sumail Fortress	$45.00	$100.00
20 Rials, #20, Sultan Qaboos bin Sa'id / Central Bank	$75.00	$150.00

	Worn	New
50 Rials, #21, Sultan Qaboos bin Sa'id / Jabreen Fort	$250.00	$375.00

1985-90 Issue

	Worn	New
100 Baisa, #22, Sultan Qaboos bin Sa'id / Port of Qaboos	$2.00	$3.50
200 Baisa, #23, Sultan Qaboos bin Sa'id / Rustaq Fort	$2.00	$4.00
1/4 Rial, #24, Sultan Qaboos bin Sa'id / Modern fishing industry	$3.25	$4.75
1/2 Rial, #25, Sultan Qaboos bin Sa'id / Sultan Qaboos University	$5.25	$7.00
1 Rial, #26, Sultan Qaboos bin Sa'id / Sohar Fort	$8.50	$10.00
5 Rials, #27, Sultan Qaboos bin Sa'id / Fort Nizwa	$27.50	$45.00
10 Rials, #28, Sultan Qaboos bin Sa'id / Fort Mirani	$55.00	$75.00
20 Rials, #29, Sultan Qaboos bin Sa'id / Central Bank	$100.00	$130.00
50 Rials, #30, Sultan Qaboos bin Sa'id / Jabreen Fort	$200.00	$300.00

1995 Issue

	Worn	New
100 Baisa, #31, Sultan Qaboos bin Sa'id / Eagle and Oryx	$1.00	$1.75
200 Baisa, #32, Sultan Qaboos bin Sa'id / Raysut Port and Sultan Qaboos Port	$1.50	$3.00

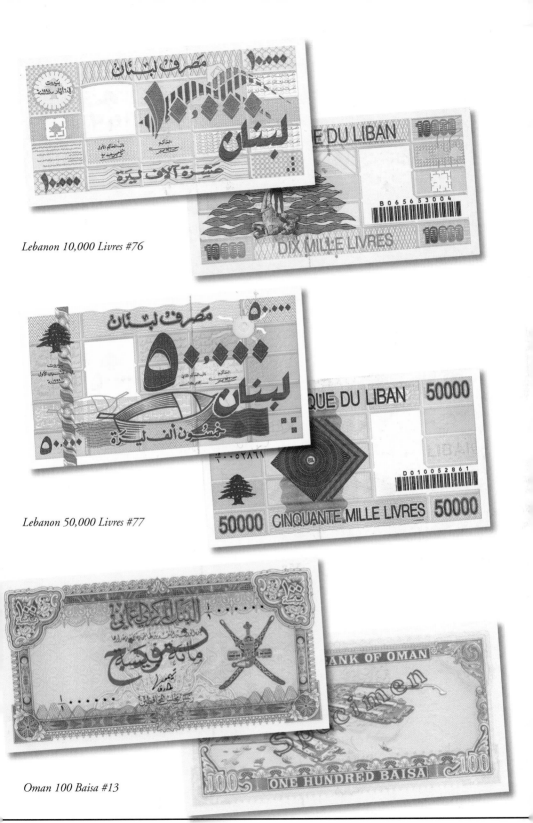

Lebanon 10,000 Livres #76

Lebanon 50,000 Livres #77

Oman 100 Baisa #13

Oman 5 Rials #18

Oman 50 Rials #21

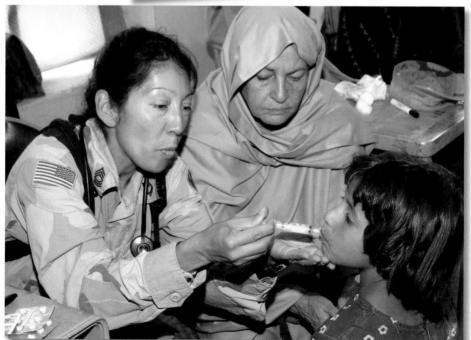

	Worn	New
1/2 Rial, #33, Sultan Qaboos bin Sa'id / Nakhl Fort	$2.50	$4.00
1 Rial, #34, Sultan Qaboos bin Sa'id / Omani Khanjar, silver bracelets and ornaments	$4.50	$7.00
5 Rials, #35, Sultan Qaboos bin Sa'id / Nizwa city view	$20.00	$35.00
10 Rials, #36, Sultan Qaboos bin Sa'id / Mutrah Fort and Corniche	$30.00	$55.00
20 Rials, #37, Sultan Qaboos bin Sa'id / Aerial view of Rysayl	$50.00	$100.00
50 Rials, #38, Sultan Qaboos bin Sa'id / Ministry of Commerge and Industry	$100.00	$225.00

2000 Issue

	Worn	New
5 Rials, #39, Sultan Qaboos bin Sa'id / Nizwa city view	$17.50	$27.50
10 Rials, #40, Sultan Qaboos bin Sa'id / Mutrah Fort and Corniche	$22.50	$45.00
20 Rials, #41, Sultan Qaboos bin Sa'id / Rysayl Industrial Area	$40.00	$85.00
50 Rials, #42, Sultan Qaboos bin Sa'id / Ministry of Commerce and Industry	$90.00	$180.00

Pakistan

Government of Pakistan

1981-present Issue

	Worn	New
1 Rupee, #25-27, Arms / Tomb of Allama Moghammed Iqbal	$0.50	$1.00

State Bank of Pakistan

1976-77 Issue

	Worn	New
5 Rupees, #28, Mohammed Ali Jinnah / Khajak railroad tunnel	$2.50	$4.00
10 Ruppes, #29, Mohammed Ali Jinnah / View of Moenjodaro	$2.50	$4.00
50 Rupees, #30, Mohammed Ali Jinnah / Main gate of Lahore fort	$5.00	$12.50
100 Rupees, #31, Mohammed Ali Jinnah/ Islamic College in Peshawar	$12.50	$25.00

1981-82 Issue

	Worn	New
5 Rupees, #33, Mohammed Ali Jinnah / Khajak railroad tunnel	$2.50	$5.00
10 Rupees, #34, Mohammed Ali Jinnah / View of Moenjodaro	$2.50	$5.00

Oman 50 Rials #30

Pakistan 100 Rupees #36

Pakistan 20 Rupees #37

Qatar 5 Riyal #8

	Worn	New
50 Rupees, #35, Mohammed Ali Jinnah / Main gate of Lahore fort	$7.50	$12.50
100 Rupees, #36, Mohammed Ali Jinnah / Islamic College in Peshawar	$12.50	$25.00

1983-88 Issue

	Worn	New
2 Rupees, #37, Arms / Badshahi mosque	$2.00	$4.00
5 Rupees, #38, Mohammed Ali Jinnah / Khajak railroad tunnel	$0.25	$1.00
10 Rupees, #39, Mohammed Ali Jinnah / View of Moenjodaro	$0.50	$1.50
50 Rupees, #40, Mohammed Ali Jinnah / Main gate of Lahore fort	$1.50	$6.00
100 Rupees, #41, Mohammed Ali Jinnah / Islamic College is Peshawar	$2.50	$7.50
500 Rupees, #42, Mohammed Ali Jinnah / State Bank of Pakistan	$10.00	$30.00
1000 Rupees, #43, Mohammed Ali Jinnah / Tomb of Jajangir	$20.00	$50.00

1997 Commemorative Issue

	Worn	New
5 Rupees, #44, Mohammed Ali Jinnah / Tomb of Shah Ruke-e-Alam	$3.50	$5.00

Qatar

Qatar Monetary Agency

1980s Issue

	Worn	New
1 Riyal, #7, Arms / Doha street scene	$0.75	$4.00
5 Riyals, #8, Arms / Sheep and plants	$2.25	$7.50
10 Riyals, #9, Arms / National Museum	$3.00	$10.00
50 Riyals, #10, Arms / Furnace at a steel factory	$15.00	$30.00
100 Riyals, #11, Arms / Qatar Monetary Agency	$30.00	$50.00
500 Riyals, #12, Arms / Offshore oil platform	$150.00	$250.00

1985 Issue

	Worn	New
1 Riyal, #13, Arms / Beached boat before Ministry of Finance and Emir's Palace	$0.50	$1.75

Qatar Central Bank

1996 Issue

	Worn	New
1 Riyal, #14, Arms / Doha street scene	$0.50	$1.00
5 Riyals, #15, Arms / Sheep and plants	$1.50	$3.50
10 Riyals, #16, Arms / National Museum	$2.50	$5.50
50 Riyals, #17, Arms / Furnace at a steel factory	$15.00	$30.00

Qatar 100 Riyals #11

Qatar 50 Riyals #17

Qatar 500 Riyals #19

Qatar 1 Riyal #20

Qatar 10 Riyals #22

U.S. ARMY PHOTO BY SGT. JEREMIAH JOHNSON

Private First Class Adam Sorenson, Tactical Psychological Operations Detatchment (TPD) out of Fort Bragg, North Carolina, hands out flyers while on patrol in Mosul, Iraq.

	Worn	New
100 Riyals, #18, Arms / Qatar Monetary Agency	$22.50	$45.00
500 Riyals, #19, Arms / Offshore oil platform	$85.00	$175.00

2003 Issue

	Worn	New
1 Riyal, #20, Arms / Three native birds	$0.50	$1.25
5 Riyals, #21, Arms / National museum and native animals	$1.25	$3.50
10 Riyals, #22, Arms / Dhow and sand dunes	$2.50	$5.00
50 Riyals, #23, Arms / Qatar Central Bank & oyster and pearl monument	$15.00	$30.00
100 Riyals, #96, Arms / Mosque of the Sheikhs & al-Shaqab Institute	$22.50	$45.00
500 Riyals, #97, Arms / Royal Palace and falcon's head	$85.00	$185.00

Saudi Arabia

Saudi Arabian Monetary Agency

1976-77 Issue

	Worn	New
1 Riyal, #16, King Faisal / Hill of Light & Airport	$0.75	$3.50
5 Riyals, #17, King Faisal / Irrigation canal & Dam	$2.00	$7.50
10 Riyals, #18, King Faisal / Oil platform & Oil refinery	$4.00	$15.00

	Worn	New
50 Riyals, #19, King Faisal / Arches of mosque at center & Courtyard of mosque	$20.00	$60.00
100 Riyals, #20, Mosque & King 'Abd al-'Aziz ibn Saud / Long building with arches	$35.00	$90.00

1983-84 Issue

	Worn	New
1 Riyal, #21, King Fahd / Flowers and landscape	$1.00	$2.00
5 Riyals, #22, King Fahd / Oil refinery	$1.50	$3.25
10 Riyals, #23, King Fahd and fortress / Palm trees	$4.00	$9.00
50 Riyals, #24, King Fahd and Dome of the Rock / Mosque	$12.50	$25.00
100 Riyals, #25, King Fahd and mosque / Mosque	$25.00	$50.00

1982-84 Issue

	Worn	New
500 Riyals, #26, King 'Abd al-'Aziz Ibn Saud / Courtyard of Great Mosque.	$90.00	$185.00

2000 Commemorative Issue

	Worn	New
20 Riyals, #27, Abdul Aziz / Annur mountain and commemorative logo	$5.00	$10.00
200 Riyals, #28, Abdul Aziz and emblem / Al-Mussmack Palace	$40.00	$85.00

2003 Issue

	Worn	New
100 Riyals, #29, King Fahd and mosque / Mosque	$20.00	$45.00
500 Riyals, #30	$90.00	$185.00

Saudi Arabian 50 Riyals #24

Saudi Arabian 20 Riyals #27

Somalia 1,000 Shilin #37

Somalia 50 N. Shilin #R2

Somalia

Central Bank of Somalia
1977 Issue

	Worn	New
5 Shilin, #20A, Gnus and zebras / Banana harvesting	$12.50	$45.00
5 Shilin, #21, Cape buffalo / Banana harvesting	$2.00	$12.50
10 Shilin, #22, Minaret / Shipbuilders	$4.00	$25.00
20 Shilin, #32, Bank building / Cattle	$7.50	$40.00
100 Shilin, #24, Woman with baby, rifle and farm tools / Workers in factory	$10.00	$70.00

1980 Issue

	Worn	New
10 Shilin, #26, Minaret / Shipbuilders	$2.50	$10.00
20 Shilin, #27, Bank building / Cattle	$5.00	$27.50
100 Shilin, #28, Woman with baby, rifle and farm tools / Workers in factory	$7.50	$30.00

1981 Issue

	Worn	New
20 Shilin, #29, Bank building at center / Cattle	$10.00	$37.50
100 Shilin, #30, Woman with baby, rifle and farm tools / Workers in factory	$7.50	$30.00

1983 Issue

	Worn	New
5 Shilin, #31, Cape buffalo herd / Banana harvesting	$0.50	$2.50
10 Shilin, #32, Lighthouse / Shipbuilding	$0.75	$3.00
20 Shilin, #33, Bank / Workers in factory	$0.50	$3.50
50 Shilin, #34, Walled city / Watering anamals	$0.50	$3.00
100 Shilin, #35, Woman with baby, rifle and farm tools / Workers in factory	$0.50	$3.00

1989 Issue

	Worn	New
500 Shilin, #36, Fisherman mending nets / Mosque	$1.50	$5.00

1990 Issue

	Worn	New
1000 Shilin, #37, Woman seated weaving baskets / Port of Mogadishu	$1.50	$3.00

1991 Mogadishu North Forces Issue

	Worn	New
20 N. Shilin, #R1, Trader leading camel / Cotton picking	$1.50	$7.00
50 N. Shilin, #R2, Man working loom / Youth leading donkey with three kids	$5.00	$15.00

Somaliland 50 Shillings #7

Yaltchin Kaya, A Turkish KBR driver that was held hostage for 10 days shakes hands with 1LT Jason Royston from 3rd Squad, 1st Platoon, 9th Engineer Battalion, attached to 1-77th Armor, 2nd Brigade, 1st Infantry Division moments after being rescued by Iraqi National Guard and US soldiers during house to house search in Samarra during recent major combat operation as part of Iraqi Freedom.

2000 Putland Regional Issue

	Worn	New
1000 Shilin, #R10, Woman seated weaving baskets / Port of Mogadishu	$1.00	$5.00

Somalliland

Baanka Somaliland

1994 Issue

	Worn	New
5 Shillings, #1, Building / Traders with camels	$0.50	$1.00
10 Shillings, #2, Building / Traders with camels	$0.50	$1.25
20 Shilnigs, #3, Building / Traders with camels	$0.75	$2.25
50 Shillings, #4, Building / Traders with camels	$1.00	$4.00
100 Shillings, #5, Building / Ship at dockside, herdsman with sheep	$2.00	$6.50
500 Shillings, #6, Building / Ship at dockside, herdsman with sheep	$8.00	$15.00

1996 Issue

	Worn	New
50 Shillings, #7, Building / Traders with camels	$0.50	$2.50
5-500 Shillings, Bronze Overprint, #8-13, Set of #1-7 with 5th Anniversary Overprint, 4 lines of text.		$50.00
5-500 Shillings, Silver overprint, #14-19, Set of #1-7 with 5th Anniversary Overprint, 2 lines of text.		$50.00

Sudan

Bank of Sudan
1981 Issue

	Worn	New
25 Piastres, #16, President J. Nimeiri / Kosti bridge	$1.00	$2.50
50 Piastres, #17, President J. Nimeiri / Bank of Sudan	$1.25	$4.50
1 Pound, #18, President J. Nimeiri / People's Assembly	$3.50	$15.00
5 Pounds, #19, President J. Nimeiri / Islamic Centre Mosque in Khartoum	$6.00	$30.00
10 Pounds, #20, President J. Nimeiri / Kenana sugar factory	$15.00	$75.00
20 Pounds, #21, President J. Nimeiri / People's Palace	$30.00	$120.00

1981 Commemorative Issue

	Worn	New
20 Pounds, #22, President J. Nimeiri / People's Palace	$22.50	$85.00

1983-84 Issue

	Worn	New
25 Piastres, #23, President J. Nimeiri / Kosti bridge	$0.50	$1.50

Somaliland 5-500 Shillings #8-13
Note Bronze overprint on face.

Somaliland 500 Shillings #18
Note silver overprint on face.

Sudan 100 Pounds #50

Sudan 50 Dinars #54

Sudan 100 Dinars #56

Sudan 200 Dinars #57

Sudan 500 Dinars #58

	Worn	New		Worn	New
50 Piastres, #24, President J. Nimeiri / Bank of Sudan	$1.25	$2.00	50 Piastres, #31, Map of Sudan & Lyre and drum / Bank of Sudan	$0.50	$2.50
1 Pound, #25, President J. Nimeiri / People's Assembly	$1.25	$2.50	1 Pound, #32, Map of Sudan & Cotton Boll / Bank of Sudan	$0.75	$3.00
5 Pounds, #26, President J. Nimeiri / Islamic Centre Mosque in Khartoum	$2.50	$12.50	5 Pounds, #33, Map of Sudan & Cattle / Bank of Sudan	$4.00	$30.00
10 Pounds, #27, President J. Nimeiri / Kenana sugar factory	$7.50	$35.00	10 Pounds, #34, Map of Sudan & City gateway / Bank of Sudan	$6.00	$45.00
20 Pounds, #28, President J. Nimeiri / People's Palace	$10.00	$55.00	20 Pounds, #35, Map of Sudan & Feluka / Bank of Sudan	$30.00	$250.00
50 Pounds, #29, President J. Nimeiri / Sailing ship and oil tanker	$20.00	$70.00	50 Pounds, #36, Map of Sudan & Columns along pool / Bank of Sudan	$30.00	$250.00

1985 Issue

1987-90 Issue

	Worn	New		Worn	New
25 Piastres, #30, Map of Sudan & Camels / Bank of Sudan	$0.40	$1.50	25 Piastres, #37, Map of Sudan & Camels / Bank of Sudan	$0.15	$0.50

Sudan 1000 Dinars #59

Sudan 200 Dinars #60

Sudan 2000 Dinars #63

	Worn	New
50 Piastres, #38, Map of Sudan & Lyre and drum / Bank of Sudan	$0.25	$0.75
1 Pound, #39, Map of Sudan & Cotton Boll / Bank of Sudan	$0.25	$1.00
5 Pounds, #40, Map of Sudan & Cattle / Bank of Sudan	$1.50	$15.00
10 Pounds, #41, Map of Sudan & City gateway / Bank of Sudan	$3.00	$30.00
20 Pounds, #42, Map of Sudan & Feluka / Bank of Sudan	$2.50	$20.00
50 Pounds, #43, Map of Sudan & Columns along pool / Bank of Sudan	$5.00	$15.00
100 Pounds, #44, Map of Sudan & University of Khartoum / Bank of Sudan	$3.00	$25.00

1991 Issue

	Worn	New
5 Pounds, #45, Map of Sudan & cattle / Bank of Sudan	$0.50	$1.75
10 Pounds, #46, Map of Sudan & City gateway / Bank of Sudan	$0.75	$2.00
20 Pounds, #47, Map of Sudan & Feluka / Bank of Sudan	$0.75	$2.50
50 Pounds, #48, Map of Sudan & Columns along pool / Bank of Sudan	$1.00	$3.50

	Worn	New
100 Pounds, #49, Map of Sudan & City gateway / Bank of Sudan-Lt. Green coin	$2.50	$17.50
100 Pounds, #50, Map of Sudan & City gateway / Bank of Sudan-Pink coin	$1.00	$2.00

1992-98 Issue

	Worn	New
5 Dinars, #51, People's Palace / Sunflowers	$0.75	$1.50
10 Dinars, #52, People's Palace / Domed building with tower	$1.50	$3.50
25 Dinars, #53, People's Palace / Circular design	$2.50	$5.00
50 Dinars, #54, People's Palace / Value	$2.50	$5.00
100 Dinars, #55, People's Palace / Building	$3.50	$7.50
100 Dinars, #56, People's Palace / Building, segmented foil security thread	$2.50	$5.00
200 Dinars, #57, People's Palace / Building	$4.00	$8.00
500 Dinars, #58, People's Palace / Oil well and building	$5.00	$10.00
1000 Dinars, #59, People's Palace / Building	$10.00	$20.00

2002-03 Issue

	Worn	New
200 Dinars, #60	$5.00	$12.50
2000 Dinars, #63, Dam and oil rig / Bank of Sudan	$12.50	$25.00

Syria 1 Pound #99

Syria 5 Pounds #100

	Worn	New
Syria		

Central Bank of Syria

1976-77 Issue

	Worn	New
1 Pound, #99, Omayyad Mosque & craftsman / Combine	$2.50	$10.00
5 Pounds, #100, Bosra theater and statue / Cotton picking and spinning frame	$1.50	$4.00
10 Pounds, #101, Al-Azem Palace in Damascus / Water treatment plant	$0.75	$1.50
25 Pounds, #102, Krak des Chevaliers castle / Central Bank	$1.00	$4.00
50 Pounds, #103, Dam / Citadel of Aleppo	$2.50	$6.00
100 Pounds, #104, Ancient Palmyra ruins / Grain silos at Lattakia	$2.50	$6.00

	Worn	New
500 Pounds, #105, Ruins of Ugarit kingdom / Ancient religious wheel and clay tablet	$7.50	$35.00

1997-98 Issue

	Worn	New
50 Pounds, #107, Aleppo Citadel & waterwheel of Hama / Al-Assad library, Abbyssian stadium	$1.00	$2.50
100 Pounds, #108, Bosra theater & Philip / Hajaz Railway locomotive, Damascus station	$2.00	$4.00
200 Pounds, #109, Monument to the Unknown soldier & statue of Saladdin / Cotton weaving and energy plant	$4.00	$7.50
500 Pounds, #110, Queen Zenobia and Palmyra theater / Eufrate dam	$10.00	$20.00
1000 Pounds, #111, Omayyad Mosque and H. Assad / Oil industry workers	$15.00	$35.00

Turkish 10,000 Lira #199

Turkish 100,000 Lira #205

Turkey

Turkiye Cumhuriyet Merkez Bankasi

1971 Issue

	Worn	New
5 Lira, #185, President Ataturk / Manavgat waterfall in Antalya	$0.50	$2.00
10 Lira, #186, President Ataturk / Maiden's Tower on the Bosphorus in Istanbul	$1.00	$4.00
20 Lira, #187, President Ataturk / Mausoleum of Ataturk in Ankara	$0.50	$1.50
50 Lira, #187A, President Ataturk / Soldier statue from Victory monument in Ankara	$4.00	$15.00
50 Lira, #188, President Ataturk / Marble fountain in Topkapi Palace in Istanbul	$0.50	$1.75

	Worn	New
100 Lira, #189, President Ataturk / Mt. Ararat	$1.00	$2.00
500 Lira, #190, President Ataturk / Main Gate of Istanbul University	$7.50	$15.00
1000 Lira, #191, President Ataturk / Bosphorus river and suspension bridge	$3.00	$10.00

1984 Issue

	Worn	New
10 Lira, #192, President Ataturk / Children presenting flowers to Ataturk, Dull Gray-Green printing	$0.20	$0.50
10 Lira, #193, President Ataturk / Children presenting flowers to Ataturk, Black printing	$0.20	$0.50
100 Lira, #194, President Ataturk / Mehmet Akif Ersoy, his home and document	$0.30	$1.25
500 Lira, #195, President Ataturk / Clock tower in Izmir	$0.50	$1.50

Turkish 250,000 Lira #211

Turkish 500,000 Lira #212

Turkish 10,000,000 Lira #214

	Worn	New		Worn	New
1000 Lira, #196, President Ataturk / Fathi Sultan Mehmet	$0.75	$1.75	50,000 Lira, #204, President Ataturk / National Parliament house in Ankara, value in gray	$0.50	$2.50
5000 Lira, #196A, President Ataturk / Mevlana Museum in Konya	$7.50	$25.00	100,000 Lira, #205, President Ataturk / Children presenting flowers to Ataturk with security device at upper right	$0.50	$6.00
5000 Lira, #197, President Ataturk / Seated Mevlana and Mevlana Museum tower	$2.50	$7.50	100,000 Lira, #206, President Ataturk with out security device	$0.50	$2.00
5000 Lira, #198, President Ataturk / Afsin-Elbistan thermal power plant	$1.25	$4.00	250,000 Lira, #207, President Ataturk / Kizilkale Fortress as Alunya	$0.50	$5.00
10,000 Lira, #199, President Ataturk / Selimiye Mosque in Edirne, Dark Green	$1.75	$5.00	500,000 Lira, #208, President Ataturk / Aerial view of Canalkale Martyrs Monument	$0.75	$7.50
10,000 Lira, #200, President Ataturk / Selimiye Mosque in Edirne, Pale Green	$0.50	$2.25	1,000,000 Lira, #209, President Ataturk / Ataturk dam in Sanliurfa	$1.00	$12.50
20,000 Lira, #201, President Ataturk / New Central Bank building	$0.50	$7.00	5,000,000 Lira, #210, President Ataturk / Antikabir building complex in Ankara	$1.00	$17.50
20,000 Lira, #202, President Ataturk / New Central Bank, Lighter colors	$0.50	$2.50	**1998 Issue**		
50,000 Lira, #203, President Ataturk / National Parliament house in Ankara	$0.50	$7.50	250,000 Lira, #211, President Ataturk / Kizilkale Fortress at Alunya	$0.50	$2.00

	Worn	New
500,000 Lira, #212, President Ataturk / Aerial view of Canakkale Martyrs Monument	$0.50	$3.50
1,000,000 Lira, #213, President Ataturk / Ataturk Dam	$0.50	$6.00
10,000,000 Lira, #214, President Ataturk / World map of 1513	$1.00	$22.50
20,000,000 Lira, #215, President Ataturk / Efes ancient city	$2.50	$37.50

2005 Issue

	Worn	New
1 New Lira, #216, President Ataturk / Ataturk Dam	$0.50	$3.00
5 New Lira, #217, President Ataturk / Mausolem of Ataturk	$2.50	$11.00
10 New Lira, #218, President Ataturk / Mausolem of Ataturk	$5.00	$20.00

	Worn	New
20 New Lira, #219, President Ataturk / Ancient city of Ephesus	$10.00	$40.00
50 New Lira, #220, President Ataturk / Goreme National Park, Capadoccia	$25.00	$75.00
100 New Lira, #221, President Ataturk / Ishak Pasha Palace, Dogu Bayazit	$50.00	$135.00

Yemen Arab Republic

Central Bank of Yemen

1979 Issue

	Worn	New
1 Rial, #16B, al-Baqiliyah Mosque / Coffee plants	$0.25	$1.00
5 Rials, #17, Dhahr al-Dahab / Fortress Qal' at al-Qahira overlooking Ta'izz	$0.75	$5.00
10 Rials, #18, Village of Thulla / Al-Baqiliyah Mosque	$2.00	$10.00

Turkish 20,000,000 Lira #215

Yemen 1 Rials #16B

Yemen 5 Rials #17

Yemen 20 Rials #19

	Worn	New		Worn	New
20 Rials, #19, Marble scuplture / View of San'a	$3.00	$12.50	50 Rials, #27A, Bronze statue of Ma'adkarib / Shibam city view	$0.75	$4.50
100 Rials, #21, al-Ashrafiya Mosque and Ta'izz / View of San'a	$5.00	$25.00	100 Rials, #28, Ancient culvert in Aden / City view of San'a	$0.50	$3.00
100 Rials, #21A, Marble scuplture of cherub and griffin / Central Bank of Yemen	$2.50	$10.00	200 Rials, #29, Alabaster sculpture / Harbor view of Mukalla	$1.25	$7.50
1990 Issue			500 Rials, #30, Central Bank of Yemen / Bara'an temple ruins	$3.00	$12.50
10 Rials, #23, Baqilyah Mosque / Ma'rib Dam with "10" at upper left and lower right	$0.50	$3.00	**1998 Issue**		
10 Rials, #24, Baqilyah Mosque / Ma'rib Dam	$0.50	$3.00	500 Rials, #31, Palace on the Rock / Al Muhdar Mosque in Tarim, Hadramaut	$3.00	$12.50
20 Rials, #25, Marble sculpture / Coastal view of Aden & dhow	$0.75	$5.00	1000 Rials, #32, Sultan's palace in Seiyem & Hadramaut / Bab al-Yemen and old city of San'a	$5.00	$20.00
20 Rials, #26, Marble sculpture / Coastal view of San'a	$3.00	$10.00	1000 Rials, #33, Sultan's palace in Seiyem & Hadramaut / Bab al-Yemen and old city of San'a with date	$5.00	$20.00
50 Rials, #27, Bronze statue of Ma'adkarib/ Shibam city view with Arabic title Shibamhadramaut	$0.75	$4.50			

Yemen 100 Rials #21

Yemen 10 Rials # 24

Yemen 20 Rials #26

Yemen 50 Rials #27A

Yemen 100 Rials #28

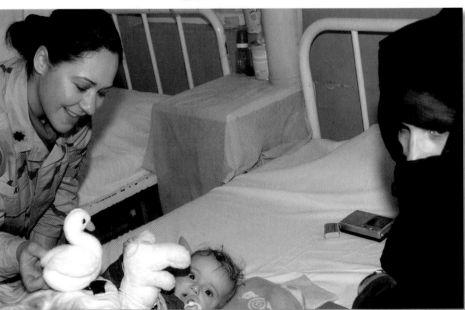

PHOTO BY SGT. 1ST CLASS DARREN D. HEUSEL, 105TH MOBILE PUBLIC AFFAIRS
DETACHMENT, OKLAHOMA ARMY NATIONAL GUARD

KABUL, Afghanistan - Lt. Col. Janet Kai a reservist from Miami, Fla., and a member of the Office of Military Cooperation-Afghanistan, brings a smile to a young child's face during a New Year's Day visit to the Indira Ghandi Children's Hospital in Kabul.

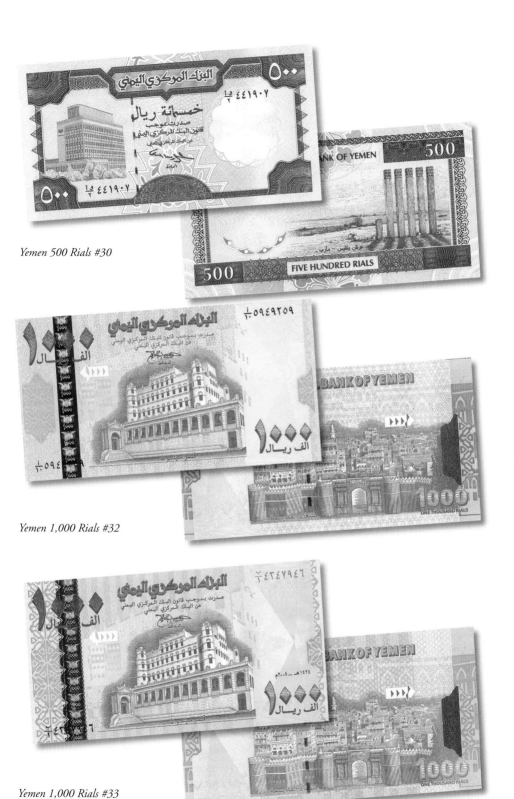

Yemen 500 Rials #30

Yemen 1,000 Rials #32

Yemen 1,000 Rials #33

Pogs

In the days when milk and juice were sold in glass bottles, round cardboard inserts with pull-tabs were used to cap them off. These caps often displayed the name of the dairy or of the specific product contained in the bottle. Back then, the Haleakala Dairy on the island of Maui, Hawaii, produced a blend of Passion fruit, Orange and Guava, which they bottled for sale. As the hobby of collecting these milk and juice caps developed over the years the acronym POG came into use, based on the Haleakala Dairy fruit drink. By the 1980's most dairies no longer used glass bottles and cardboard caps, but an avid collecting public had grown up around these little advertising pieces and POGs were poised to hit mainstream pop culture.

During the 1990's POGs developed into a cultural phenomenon, with new POGs being made for collecting and games being invented to promote new uses for the little cardboard discs. Now with blazing colors and radical designs, the new POGs seldom displayed advertising, never had pull-tabs and had distanced themselves from their humble, yet practical, dairy beginnings. In 1993 the World POG Federation was formed to standardize the various games, but within ten years the sensation was almost completely forgotten and POGs had slipped away from public consciousness. The third re-birth of POGs was brewing however and this time they would return to a very practical use.

In the military, troops serving outside the United States were often paid in Military Payment Certificates. These specialized banknotes were used from 1946-1973. This was done to limit servicemen's spending to on-base locations and to decrease the risk of large amounts of real U.S. currency being obtained by the enemy. With the downsizing of military personnel overseas after the Vietnam War Era, U.S. Currency, and more often debit cards came into use for base exchanges during times of peace.

For the expansion during Operation Iraqi Freedom and Operation Enduring Freedom, the United States Army & Air Force Exchange Service (AAFES) needed small change at overseas locations but due to the expense of shipping coins, decided to print circular discs to serve the purpose. These new colorful discs, known as Gift Certificates, are in effect the 21st century rebirth of the decades old POG. As a plus, these new POGs have regained a very practical use, this time as a working currency for the military.

5 cent Pog

CPT Brian Barber, right, and SSG Schweighauber, both with 1st Battalion, 8th Infantry Regiment, Headquarters, Headquarters Command, 3rd Brigade Combat Team, 4th Infantry Division, out of Fort Carson, Colorado, discuss their current position relative to the location where they should be on the morning of Oct. 10, 2003. They were setting up check points near Balad, Iraq. The soldiers are deployed in support of Operation Iraqi Freedom, the multinational coalition effort to liberate the Iraqi people and end the regime of Saddam Hussein.

These new currency discs are printed in Dallas Texas, near where the Headquarters of the AAFES is located. The staff of the AAFES selects the images of people and equipment pictured on the POGs. They insist that they are not to be used as currency or Military Payment Certificates outside of the AAFES Exchange system, though many have found their way into the hands of POG collectors back home in the U.S.

As of spring 2005 there have been six groups issued. Starting in 2003, dates were incorporated on the top of the discs. Some display the Operational names; many have pictures of personnel or equipment. All have a face value or denomination printed on one side and a picture on the other. Some of the more recent issues have also pictured service personnel from other eras, such as World War II and the Vietnam War. Additional information on these denominated discs can be located at the private web site www.aafespogs.com.

1st Series

5 cent Pog

10 cent Pog

25 cent Pog

	New
1st Series	
5 Cents, Large value in red on both sides	**$1.00**
10 Cents, Large value in blue on both sides	**$2.00**
25 Cents, Large value in white on both sides	**$3.00**
2nd Series	
5 Cents, in white on blue background, A-10 Thunderbolt II	**$0.50**
5 Cents, B-2 Spirit	**$0.50**
5 Cents, Patriot missile truck	**$0.50**
5 Cents, Paratroopers	**$0.50**
5 Cents, B-52 Stratofortress	**$0.50**
5 Cents, A-7 Corsair II	**$0.50**

	New
5 Cents, AH -64 Apache	**$0.50**
5 Cents, Operation Iraqi Freedom in Clouds	**$0.50**
5 Cents, Two F-15, sun in background	**$0.50**
5 Cents, Two F-15, one banking	**$0.50**
5 Cents, Dolphin / Porpoise	**$0.50**
5 Cents, CH-47 Chinook transporting tank	**$0.50**
10 Cents, in white on tan background, AC-130 Spectre front view	**$1.00**
10 Cents, Two F-16 Fighting Falcons	**$1.00**
10 Cents, Two H-60, Black Hawk and CH-47 Chinook	**$1.00**
10 Cents, Surface-to-air missile launcher	**$1.00**
10 Cents, F-15 Eagle in banking turn	**$1.00**

2nd Series

5 cent Pog

10 cent Pog

10 cent Pog

10 cent Pog

25 cent Pog

	New		**New**
10 Cents, Warheads on bombs	$1.00	25 Cents, Close-up of soldier wearing gas mask	$2.00
10 Cents, Two soldiers wearing gas masks	$1.00	25 Cents, UH-1 Iroquois advancing forward	$2.00
10 Cents, Troops around anti-aircraft gun	$1.00	25 Cents, E-3 Sentry AWACS	$2.00
10 Cents, Battleship firing	$1.00	25 Cents, Pilot in cockpit of F-16 Fighting falcon as seen from above	$2.00
10 Cents, Four pilots being assisted into F-15 Eagle	$1.00		
10 Cents, Soldier aiming a gun	$1.00	25 Cents, Operation Iraqi Freedom, top of vehicle	$2.00
10 Cents, Tank advancing right	$1.00	25 Cents, Radar installation	$2.00
25 Cents, In white on orange background, CH-46 Sea Knight helicopter	$2.00	25 Cents, F/A-18 Hornet as seen from below	$2.00
		25 Cents, MOAB Missile	$2.00
25 Cents, F-16 Fighting Falcondiving	$2.00	25 Cents, H-60 with solder on exit ladder	$2.00
		25 Cents, Jeep	$2.00

3rd Series

5 cent Pog

10 cent Pog

10 cent Pog

25 cent Pog

25 cent Pog

3rd Series	New		New
5 Cents, In white on blue background, 2003 added, soldier inspecting mouth of child	$0.50	5 Cents, KC-10 Extender refueling F/A-22 Raptor	$0.50
		5 Cents, F/A-18 Hornet	$0.50
5 Cents, Soldier seated in vehicle, flag behind	$0.50	10 Cents, in white on tan background, AH-640 Apache-Longbow	$0.50
5 Cents, Soldier standing by flag	$0.50	10 Cents, Child's face and flag	$0.50
5 Cents, Child hugging soldier	$0.50	10 Cents, Soldier and flag	$0.50
5 Cents, Soldier wearing oxygen mask	$0.50	10 Cents, Jet fighter in flight, airstream behind	$0.50
5 Cents, H-3 Sea King and soldier	$0.50	10 Cents, View over pilot's shoulder, F-16 Fighting Falcon	$1.00
5 Cents, Amphibious transport	$0.50		
5 Cents, Statue of Liberty and HH-65 Dolphin	$0.50	10 Cents, Soldier left, rock pile in background	$1.00
5 Cents, Soldier at BX/PX store	$0.50	10 Cents, Flair of a rocket	$1.00
5 Cents, Proudly serving those who serve, flag background	$0.50	10 Cents, Seated soldier with shoulder missile launcher	$1.00

4th Series

5 cent Pog

10 cent Pog

10 cent Pog

25 cent Pog

25 cent Pog

	New		New
10 Cents, Soldier looking down barrel of weapon	$1.00	25 Cents, Soldier inspecting child's ear	$2.00
10 Cents, Soldier with machine gun on H-60 Blawk Hawk	$1.00	25 Cents, Two C-130 Hercules on runway	$2.00
10 Cents, Amphibious tank	$1.00	25 Cents, USGC Barque Eagle	$2.00
10 Cents, C-130 Hercules dumping red liquid during flight	$1.00	25 Cents, Operation Enduring Freedom, Soldier at console	$2.00
25 Cents, in white on Orange background, Silhouette of Soldier with machine gun	$2.00	25 Cents, American Flag on deck of Aircraft Carrier	$2.00
		25 Cents, Two marines in dress uniform	$2.00
25 Cents, Silhouette of Soldier with mounted machine gun	$2.00	**4th Series**	
25 Cents, Soldier saluting flag	$2.00	5 Cents, F-35 Flying right	$0.50
25 Cents, AV-8B Harrier jets on approach	$2.00	5 Cents, Sailor holding child	$0.50
25 Cents, Silhouette of Solder on vehicle	$2.00	5 Cents, Two figures	$0.50
25 Cents, V-22 Osprey	$2.00	5 Cents, CH-47 Chinook transporting cargo in net	$0.50

5th Series

5 cent Pog

5 cent Pog

10 cent Pog

10 cent Pog

25 cent Pog

25 cent Pog

25 cent Pog

	New		**New**
5 Cents, B-17 Flying Fortress	$0.50	10 Cents, Soldier seated in building	$1.00
5 Cents, Pilot	$0.50	10 Cents, Soldier pointing	$1.00
5 Cents, Sailor walking toward row of flags	$0.50	10 Cents, Two soldiers in desert	$1.00
5 Cents, Soldier facing, looking thru gun	$0.50	10 Cents, Navy ship superstructure and flag	$1.00
5 Cents, Female	$0.50	10 Cents, H-60 Blawk Hawk approaching	$1.00
5 Cents, Three soldiers	$0.50	10 Cents, Operation Enduring Freedom, oil well smoke	$1.00
5 Cents, Troops landing on amphibious craft	$0.50	10 Cents, Tank left	$1.00
5 Cents, Guard tower silhouette	$0.50	10 Cents, Five pilots by plane	$1.00
10 Cents, Soldier standing left, holding machine gun	$1.00	10 Cents, Two soldiers near flaming item	$1.00

6th Series

5 cent Pog

25 cent Pog

25 cent Pog

25 cent Pog

25 cent Pog

	New		**New**
10 Cents, Cockpit of B-1B Lancer	**$1.00**	25 Cents, Machine Gunner on Humvee	**$2.00**
10 Cents, H-60 Blawk Hawk on Aircraft carrier	**$1.00**	25 Cents, Operation Enduring Freedom, C-130 Hercules	**$2.00**
25 Cents, Two soldiers helping third	**$2.00**	25 Cents, Operation Iraqi Freedom, soldier with machine gun	**$2.00**
25 Cents, U.S. Coast Guard boat, under canopy	**$2.00**	25 Cents, H-60 Blawk Hawk above soldier in the desert	**$2.00**
25 Cents, Soldier seated with sandbags	**$2.00**	**5th Series**	
25 Cents, Child with small flag	**$2.00**	5 Cents, Proudly serving those who serve. Truck and plane	**$0.50**
25 Cents, Five WWII era pilots	**$2.00**	5 Cents, Soldiers lined up	**$0.50**
25 Cents, WWII era sub officer looking thru periscope	**$2.00**	5 Cents, BX/PX view	**$0.50**
25 Cents, AV-BB Harrier Rifting off from Carrier deck	**$2.00**	5 Cents, Flight Deck officer sending off P-51 Mustang	**$0.50**
25 Cents, Ship #63	**$2.00**	5 Cents, HH-53 Jolly Green Giant in flight	**$0.50**

	New		**New**
5 Cents, F-86 Sabre accending skyward	$0.50	10 Cents, Sailor greeting young daughter	$1.00
5 Cents, Soldier with building in background	$0.50	10 Cents, Soldier seated with rifle in field	$1.00
5 Cents, Operation Iraqi Freedom, H-60 Blawk Hawk and sunset	$0.50	10 Cents, Humvee approaching	$1.00
5 Cents, Five TBM Avengers bombers in formation	$0.50	25 Cents, KC-B5 Stratotanker refueling F-16 Fighting Falcon	$2.00
5 Cents, Five Jets F-15E Strike Eagles, F-15 Eagle, F-16 Fighting falconin formation	$0.50	25 Cents, B-1B Lancer flying away	$2.00
5 Cents, Naval vessel	$0.50	25 Cents, Soldier standing next to flag	$2.00
5 Cents, Capt. Charles Yeager with Bell XS-1	$0.50	25 Cents, F-16 falcons, VSAF "Thunderbirds" in formation	$2.00
10 Cents, Crew of B-29 Super Fortress Enola Gay	$1.00	25 Cents, Three soldiers under wing tuskeegee airmen	$2.00
10 Cents, Soldier with infant	$1.00	25 Cents, F/A Hornet crossing the sound barrier	$2.00
10 Cents, Crew member on flight deck, F-14 Tomcat	$1.00	25 Cents, Humvee in rearview - Operation Enduring Freedom	$2.00
10 Cents, Guard tower and razor wire	$1.00	25 Cents, WASPS in front of B-17 Flying Fortress	$2.00
10 Cents, Soldier silhouette with night vision scope	$1.00	25 Cents, Flag raising on Iwo Jima	$2.00
10 Cents, 4-B-24 Liberator in flight	$1.00	25 Cents, Man and dog	$2.00
10 Cents, Soldiers boarding rear of C-130 Hercules	$1.00	25 Cents, B-17 Flying Fortress and crew	$2.00
10 Cents, Pilot standing before F-4 Phantom II	$1.00	25 Cents, Operation Iraqi Freedom, pilot polishing plane	$2.00
10 Cents, Soldier with goggles and chains	$1.00		

A local Iraqi girl shows her enthusiasm for the United States of America (USA) being in Iraq, with a homemade sign. Her family waits to find if one of their relatives is among the thousands of Enemy Prisoners of War (EPW) held in a nearby EPW camp, captured during Operation Iraqi Freedom. Operation Iraqi Freedom is the multinational coalition effort to liberate the Iraqi people, eliminate Iraqs weapons of mass destruction and end the regime of Saddam Hussein.

6th Series

	New
5 Cents, P-51 Mustang plane	$0.50
5 Cents, Two soldiers, one seated one kneeling	$0.50
5 Cents, B-17 Flying Fortress and crew	$0.50
5 Cents, A-10 Thunderbolt II in the sky, seen from below	$0.50
5 Cents, Soldier looking in hillside hole	$0.50
5 Cents, Air Force One VC-25 in flight	$0.50
5 Cents, OH-58 Kiowa Warrior, sun behind	$0.50
5 Cents, Operation Iraqi Freedom, Soldier kneeling with gun	$0.50
5 Cents, Operation Enduring Freedom, Two soldiers walking	$0.50
5 Cents, CH-46 Sea Knight dropping out supplies	$0.50
5 Cents, Two soldiers launching mortar	$0.50
5 Cents, Smiling soldier in shirt and hat	$0.50
10 Cents, CH-47 Chinook in desert, soldier with gun	$1.00
10 Cents, Six soldiers outside large tent	$1.00
10 Cents, HH-65 Dolphin in flight	$1.00
10 Cents, Soldier in uniform leaning left	$1.00
10 Cents, Solder advancing between vertical opening	$1.00
10 Cents, Soldier leaning against wall	$1.00

	New
10 Cents, Navy Football - Midshipman	$1.00
10 Cents, Air Force Football - Falcons	$1.00
10 Cents, Army Football - Black Knights	$1.00
10 Cents, Soldier sitting with child	$1.00
10 Cents, Soldier walking amongst confiscated weapons	$1.00
10 Cents, Three soldiers advancing with weapons pointed	$1.00
25 Cents, Female sailor and young child	$2.00
25 Cents, Soldier profile clutching rifle	$2.00
25 Cents, Submarine tower	$2.00
25 Cents, Tank	$2.00
25 Cents, B-1B Lancer before Pyramids	$2.00
25 Cents, Red Cross H-60 Blawk Hawk	$2.00
25 Cents, Soldier standing before Humvee	$2.00
25 Cents, SR-71 Black Bird seen from above	$2.00
25 Cents, U.S. Army Nascar	$2.00
25 Cents, F/A-18 Hornet takeoff from aircraft carrier	$2.00
25 Cents, Allies, flag montage	$2.00
25 Cents, Proudly serving those who serve, soldiers with banner	$2.00

SERVICE AND COMMEMORATIVE MEDALS

MILITARY MEDALS

Militaries around the world have awarded medals for over 200 years to their troops for basic service as well as for exceptional dedication and courage.

While various badges, pins and patches are used to identify units and ranks many medals tend to cross over divisions and even military branches.

Campaign medals, for instance, are issued to every service member from any branch of the service, who participated in a particular campaign. Participants from the Army, Navy, Air Force and Marines, who fought in or occupied Afghanistan all would have had the opportunity to earn the same type of Afghanistan Campaign medal pictured in this chapter.

Good conduct and other exemplary service medals are usually unique to the branch of service, with the designs often differing substantially between the branches. Since these are not tied to a campaign or conflict directly we have not attempted to list them in this chapter. Similarly, we will not be displaying any of the long awarded medals of valor and merit such as Good Conduct, Purple Heart, Air Medal, Bronze and Silver Stars and Medal of Honor.

All United Nations medals look basically the same, but have different ribbons for each peacekeeping operation. For some peace keeping operations bars displaying the acronym of the mission are attached to the ribbon. In our listings we have tried to give accurate ribbon color descriptions for stripes running left to right on U.N. medals.

For all the medals listed in this chapter we have tried to mention any basic requirements or time frame of service required for their awarding. We have also attempted to give a brief description for the more unusual medals listed, especially those of other nations and those few political badges or medals from Iraq that we have chosen to list here.

We have only illustrated full size medals in this section. There are also miniature versions of almost all of these medals, which are sometimes worn for formal occasions. Matching ribbon bars, which are often worn on the regular

Saudi Arabian Medal for the Liberation of Kuwait in case with ribbon bar, value $22.00.

dress uniform, are not illustrated in this section. While all of these items have value to those who earn them, most are of limited value to collectors.

The United States stopped numbering campaign medals in 1917 and during times of war the services do not normally have time to engrave recipients names, so the majority of medals available to today's collector market, weather issued or purchased are not named or numbered. Many available medals are excess productions sold privately by the manufacturers. It is important to remember however, that a medal or group of medals will always be more highly prized by collectors if they have been engraved with the recipients name and are accompanied by official documentation. Additional relevant paper ephemera, such as citations, photographs or letters will also increase the group's desirability and value.

Many military veterans may be entitled to receive medals from the U.S. government. To determine if you have earned any campaign medals, send your branch of service, name, serial number, unit(s), dates of service and a letter requesting any medals to which you are entitled to the following address:

National Personnel Records Center
9700 Page Blvd.
St. Louis, MO 63132-5100

Be patient, as it can take up to a year for your request to be processed.

Afghanistan Campaign medal issued for U.S. participation from October 2001, value $12.50 without ribbon bar.

	Value
United States	
South West Asia Service, participation in and support of Desert Shield and Desert Storm 1991- present, with ribbon bar	$14.50
Kuwaiti Medal Liberation of Kuwait, participation in and support of Desert Shield and Desert Storm 1990-1993, with ribbon bar	$25.00
Saudi Arabian Medal for the Liberation of Kuwait, participation in and support of Desert Storm, with ribbon bar	$22.00
Liberation of Kuwait, service and support 1990-2000, with ribbon bar	$10.00
Liberation of Afghanistan, service and direct support, with ribbon bar	$10.00
Afghanistan Campaign, service in Afghanistan from October 24, 2001 to present, with ribbon bar	$14.50
Global War on Terror Service, service during the Global War on Terror, in US and overseas, with ribbon bar	$10.00
Global War on Terrorism Expeditionary, Post September 11, 2001 deployment overseas in support of the Global War on Terrorism, with ribbon bar	$10.00

	Value
Global War on Terrorism Service, Post September 11, 2001 service in US or overseas in support of the Global War on Terrorism, with ribbon bar	$10.00
Operation Iraqi Freedom, service and direct support, with ribbon bar	$10.00
Iraq Campaign, 2003-present, with ribbon bar	$14.50
United Nations	
First Emergency Force Egypt Israel, service to UNEFI, with ribbon bar	$16.50
Lebanon Observation, service to UNOGIL 1958, blue and white ribbon	$15.00
Iran & Iraq Military Observer Group, at least 90 days participation in UNIIMOG 1988-1991, blue, red, white, green and black ribbon	$16.50
Palestine Truce Supervisory Organization, serive to UNTSO, blue and white ribbon	$15.00
Secretary General Afghanistan Pakistan, service to OSGAP, with OSGAP bar	$17.50
Indian-Pakistan Observation, blue white and green ribbon	$16.50
Iraq-Kuwait Observation Mission, 90 days service to UNIKOM 1991-present, yellow and blue ribbon	$12.50

U.S. AIR FORCE PHOTO BY PRISCILLA ROBINSON

Vincenza's 173rd Army Airborne Brigade Rangers step off of a C-17 at Aviano Air Base, Italy, Feb. 20, 2004, after spending nearly a year deployed to Iraq in support of Operation Iraqi Freedom.

Global War on Terrorism expeditionary forces, post September 11, 2001, value $14.50 with ribbon bar.

Other Nations	Value
Iraq-Iran War, service 1980-1988, black and red ribbon	$25.00
Russian Invasion of Afghanistan, For Gratitude to the Afghanistan People, 1978-1988, blue ribbon with cloisonne flags	$65.00
Russian Invasion of Afghanistan, For International Friendship - 1978-1988, red ribbon with cloionne star design	$35.00
Russian Invasion of Afghanistan, service in Afghanistan 1979-1988, with official presentation booklet, blue and yellow ribbon	$50.00
Russian Afghanistan, For Veterans of International service including Afghanistan, rainbow ribbon, medal with red cloisonne	$25.00
Iraq-Iran War, Presented for civilian war assistance 1983, suspended from bar, woman and child at center	$12.00
Iraq-Iran War, Presented for civilian service during war 1983, suspended from bar, palm tree at center	$10.00
Iraq-Iran War, Wounded in service 1980-1988, red and white ribbon	$30.00

	Value
Italy Persian Gulf War, participation Persian Gulf War (manufactured by Spink & Son Ltd.), Yellow, red, green and white ribbon	$15.00
Saudi Arabian Gallantry Medal, service during Gulf War 1990-1991, Red, yellow and green ribbon	$20.00
Bahrain Kuwait Liberation, participation 1990-2000, green, white, black and red ribbon	$25.00
Iraq, al-Baath Party badge, gold colored with cloisonne	$15.00
Iraq, Victory Day badge, painted red, black, blue and white	$10.00
Iraq Nut al-Istihqaq al-'Aail, Given for bravery 1992-1993, white and blue ribbon, cloisonne medal	$12.50
Iraq Gulf War, service in the Gulf War 1991, Red, black, white and green ribbon	$28.00
Iraq, service in Sharah 'Umm al-M'aarak (Desert Storm), cloisonne medal	$15.00
Polish Stabilization forces in Iraq, Polish Command - Multinational Division Central South, military merit and service 2004-2005, Red, white and black ribbon	$50.00

Global War on Terrorism service medal for
U.S. or overseas support, value $10.00.

Iraq Campaign medal, War on Iraq 2003-
present, value $12.50 without ribbon bar.

Issued for UN Peace Keepers in Lebanon, 1958 UNOGIL. All UN Peace Keeper medals look the same, it is the ribbon which indicates the mission, time and place of service.

Iraqi al-Baath Party badge suspended from bar and cloisonné flag pendant, value $15.00.

Iraqi medal for service during the Iraq-Iran War 1980-1988, value $25.00.

UN

IN THE SERVICE OF PEACE

A soldier from the Asadabad Provincial Reconstrution Team of the Combined Joint Civil Military Operations Task Force, is greeted by a little boy in Manoi, Afghanistan on January 14, 2005.

Wounded in service medal for Iraqi participants in the Iraq-Iran War. The medal displays a red and white Russian style folded ribbon, value $30.00.

Italian medal issued for service in the Persian Gulf War, value $15.00.

GOLFO PERSICO

A US Army CH-47 helicopter flies over Baghdad, Iraq, during a distinguished visitor flight in support of Operation Iraqi Freedom, July 20, 2003. Operation Iraqi Freedom is a multi-national coalition effort to liberate the Iraqi people, eliminate Iraq's weapons of mass destruction and the regime of Saddam Hussein.

Kuwait Liberation
medal issued
by Bahrain for
participation 1990-2000,
value $25.00.

Gulf War service medal for
Gallantry issued for Saudi Arabian
participants, value $20.00.

Spc. Lamar Hudson with Bravo
Company, 34th Infantry Regiment,
1st Infantry Division from Fort Riley,
Kan., play a game of soccer with
kids on the first day of the schools'
reopening, Be Summia, for girls and
Be Smia, for boys, Feb. 7, 2004, in
Ramadi, Iraq.

U.S. ARMY PHOTO BY SGT. LEE DAVIS

Russian industrial medal issued for Service in Afghanistan 1979-1988, value $35.00.

Awarded to Russian Veterans of International service in North Korea, Cuba, Near East, Vietnam and Afghanistan, value 25.00.

Victory Day badge, awarded during early days of the first Gulf War, value $10.00.

Nepal overseas service medal, along with a UN Peace Keepers Medal for Lebanon, 1978 UNIFIL service. These two have been privately sewn together onto one board with a single pin on back.

Russian medal created to commemorate International Friendship, which saw distribution during the Communist period in Afghanistan 1978-1988, value $35.00.

Russian medal given to supporters of the pro-Soviet Military coup established Democratic Republic of Afghanistan, with official booklet, set value $65.00.

УДОСТОВЕРЕНИЕ К МЕДАЛИ
„ВОИНУ - ИНТЕРНАЦИОНАЛИСТУ
ОТ БЛАГОДАРНОГО
АФГАНСКОГО НАРОДА"

дакورنۍ نوم   ГРОМОВ
Фамилия

نوم   БОРИС
Имя

دپلار نوم   ВСЕВОЛОДОВИЧ
Отчество

نمبر   3/88
№

تاريخ   28 декабря 1988
Дата

РЕСПУБЛИКА АФГАНИСТАН

В соответствии с Указом
Президента Республики Афганистан
от „ 28 " декабря 1988 г.
награжден медалью
„ВОИНУ - ИНТЕРНАЦИОНАЛИСТУ
ОТ БЛАГОДАРНОГО
АФГАНСКОГО НАРОДА"

Booklet for above medal.

CHALLENGE COINS

The history of the Challenge Coin is steeped in legend. Some stories date it's origin to WWI, some to the Korean War and some to the Vietnam War. The purpose of the Challenge Coin in all cases however, remains the same; to foster moral and instill pride in ones service and unit.

The earliest known example of a Challenge Coin in existence today dates to the Korean War, but wide issuance of these types of medals did not occur until the Vietnam War. During the Vietnam War the traditions of always carrying your Challenge Coin and of challenging for drinks grew to widespread practice with service personnel.

In the last 20 years the practice of issuing Challenge Coins has grown tremendously, with both privately produced commercial coins available and Commander issued Unit coins being commissioned and awarded for exemplary service. Commercial Challenge Coins can be purchased on many Internet sites and are available for every branch of service. Commander commissioned Challenge Coins are normally awarded within the Unit and are prized by the recipient to the extent that they are far less often sold, traded or given away. When commissioned unit coins do eventually get sold they usually trade at higher values than the more ordinary commercial types.

We have grouped the Challenge Coin listings into the two categories of commercial and commissioned. The listings and images presented in the commercial area are products of the Northwest Territorial Mint. As the production of Challenge Coins today is so great and the issues so plentiful that an extensive listing of both commissioned and commercial issues would have been impossible to compile at this time, we have chosen to offer a representative grouping of each type. Additional information on challenge coins can be had from the private web site www.militarycoins.com.

Colorized Enduring Freedom Commercial Challenge Coin, Army Reserve.

SGT Manuel Herrera and PV2 Rittin from San Antonio, TX with the 277th Engineering Company, 420th Engineering Brigade in San Antonio, TX carefully monitor their course as they lay asphalt while expanding the taxiway at Balad Air Base on Camp Anaconda, Iraq.

Commercial Challenge Coins

	Value
Air Force	
Air Force J.R.O.T.C.	**$12.50**
Air Force seal, uniface	**$12.50**
Air National Guard	**$12.50**
Air National Guard Family	**$12.50**
Aircraft Maintenance, Military figure	**$12.50**
Aircraft Maintenance, Military figure, flag and crossed wrenches	**$12.50**
Airman (Officer)	**$12.50**
Chief Master Sergeant	**$12.50**
Civil Air Patrol, 60th Anniversary, antique finish	**$12.50**
Civil Air Patrol, 60th Anniversary, proof finish	**$12.50**
Command Chief Master Sergeant	**$12.50**
First Sergeant (one patch)	**$12.50**
First Sergeant (three patches)	**$12.50**
Grade officer (Captain)	**$12.50**
Military Spouse	**$12.50**

	Value
NCO (Staff and Technical Sergeant)	**$12.50**
NCO Creed	**$12.50**
Operation Desert Storm, 1991	**$15.00**
Operation Iraqi Freedom, antique finish, new emblem	**$12.50**
Operation Iraqi Freedom, antique finish, old emblem	**$12.50**
Operation Iraqi Freedom, proof finish, new emblem	**$12.50**
Operation Iraqi Freedom, proof finish, old emblem	**$12.50**
Skunk Works, F-117	**$12.50**
Skunk Works, F-22	**$12.50**
Skunk Works, SR-71	**$12.50**
Skunk Works, U-2	**$12.50**
SNCO (Chief or Senior Master Sergeant)	**$12.50**
Thunderbirds (Proof finish)	**$17.50**
Top 3, Chief Master, Senior Master and Master Sergeant	**$12.50**
Top 3, same as above, highlights polished.	**$15.00**
U.S. Air Force	**$12.50**
Well Done	**$12.50**

147 Fighter Wing - Houston TX   CAP 60th Anniversary

	Value		Value
Army		Quartermaster Corps	$15.00
Army National Guard	$12.50	Rangers lead the way	$12.50
Army National Guard Family	$12.50	Sergeant First Class	$12.50
Army seal, uniface	$12.50	Sergeant Major	$12.50
Command Sergeant Major	$12.50	Tank, flag and two soldiers.	$12.50
Drill Sergeant, large emblem	$12.50	Warrant Officer	$15.00
Drill Sergeant, two men flanking emblem	$15.00	**Coast Guard**	
Emblem	$12.50	50th Anniversary, proof finish	$12.50
Great Seal - Operation Noble Eage, Iraqi Freedom, Enduring Freedom, 50mm	$15.00	Emblem colored	$12.50
		Emblem, antique finish	$12.50
Master Sergeant	$12.50	USCGC Eagle, antique finish	$12.50
Military Spouse	$12.50	USCGC Eagle, proof finish	$12.50
NCO Creed with Department of the Army emblem	$12.50	**Dept. of Defense**	
NCO Creed with eagle and stripes	$12.50	Armed Forces Day, 50th Anniversary	$12.50
Operation Enduring Freedom, Let's Roll	$15.00	Joint Staff seal, uniface	$12.50
Operation Iraqi Freedom, antique finish	$12.50	Joint Staff seal, uniface	$15.00
Operation Iraqi Freedom, proof finish	$12.50	Pentagon 50th Anniversary	$15.00

Marine Corps	Value
Flag Raising on Iwo Jima	$12.50
Freedom is Never Free	$12.50
Marine Corps seal, uniface	$12.50
Military Spouse	$12.50
NCO Creed	$12.50
Once a Marine….	$12.50
Operation Iraqi Freedom, antique finish	$12.50
Operation Iraqi Freedom, proof finish	$12.50
Sergeant Major	$12.50
Tun Tavern, antique finish 1-1/2 inch	$12.50
Tun Tavern, antique finish 1-7/8 inch	$17.50
Tun Tavern, proof finish 1-1/2 inch	$12.50
Tun Tavern, proof finish 1-7/8 inch	$17.50
USMC Creed	$12.50

Navy	Value
Blue Angels, proof finish	$12.50
Chief Petty Officer	$12.50
Military Spouse	$12.50
Navy Emblem, golden	$12.50
Navy Emblem, silvered	$12.50
Navy seal, uniface	$12.50
Navy Supply Corps	$12.50
NCO Creed	$12.50
Operation Iraqi Freedom, antique finish	$12.50
Operation Iraqi Freedom, proof finish	$12.50
Operation Noble Eagle, George Bush quote	$12.50
Seabees, Chief	$12.50
Submarine Service Centennial, antique finish	$12.50
Submarine Service Centennial, proof finish	$12.50

Coalation Flags on Iraqi Feedom obverse   *USCGC Eagle Commercial issue*

Operation Noble Eagle Standardized Tactical Entry Point

Commercial Desert Storm issue

Combat Logistical
Support Squadron
Hill, AFB

1-41st Medics

909th Adjutant Gerneral Postal
detachments joint postal mission

Capt. David Minascheck, civil affairs officer for 3-82 Field Artillery, offers a backpack and a handshake
to Iraqi primary school children in Al Mansour, Oct. 9, as a part of Operation Virtual Pencil. The
Soldiers gave out 1100 backpacks that day.

*9th Engr
Batallion*

*JR ROTC
commercial coin*

TAn F/A-18 Hornet from the Mighty Shrikes of Strike Fighter Squadron Ninety Four (VFA-94) leaves a contrail while conducting missions over Iraq. Contrails form when hot humid air from jet exhaust mixes with environmental air of low vapor pressure and low temperature. The mixing is a result of turbulence generated by the engine exhaust.

U.S.S. Iwo Jima

U.S.S. Saipan

*Navy Supply Corps.
Commercial issue*

*Army Rangers
Commercial issue*

Commissioned Challenge Coins

Air Force	Value
649 CLSS Combat Logistics Support Squadron, Hill AFB Utah	$15.00
Anthony J. DeLuca, Director's Award	$20.00
Eric Benden, Chief Master Sgt.	$20.00
F. Whitten Peters, Secretary	$25.00
General Handy, Vice Chief of Staff	$25.00
General Ryan, Chief of Staff	$25.00

Army	Value
1-41st Medics	$15.00
9th Engineer Battilon, B Co.	$15.00
General Gordon Sullivan, Chief of Staff	$20.00
General Keane, Vice Chief of Staff	$20.00
General Reimer, Chief of Staff	$20.00
General Shinseki, Chief of Staff	$20.00
Joe Reeder, Under Secretary	$20.00
Louis Caldera, Secretary	$25.00
Michael P.W. Stone, Secretary	$20.00
Robert E. Hall, Sgt. Major	$20.00
Thomas White, Secretary	$20.00
Togo D. West, Jr. Secretary	$25.00

Coast Guard	Value
USCG Electronic Systems Support Unit	$15.00
USCGC Mellon WHEC 717	$15.00
Vince Patton, Master Chief Petty Officer	$20.00

Defense Dept.	Value
William Cohen, Secretary	$20.00
William Perry, Secretary	$20.00

Joint Chiefs	Value
General Colin Powell, Chairman	$25.00
General Ralson, Vice Chairman	$20.00
General Richard B. Myers, Vice Chairman	$20.00
General Shali, Chairman	$20.00
General Shelton, Chairman	$20.00

Joint Mission	Value
909th Adjutant General Postal Detachments	$15.00
Operation Noble Eagle, Standardized Tactical Entry Point	$15.00
Who's your Baghadaddy?	$15.00

Marine Corps	Value
25th Marine Regiment, 20th Marine Division	$15.00
General Jones, Commandant	$20.00
General Krulak, Commandant	$20.00
General Neal, Assistant Commandant	$20.00
Sgt. Major, USMC	$15.00

National Guard	Value
1249 Eng Battalion, Company A. Oregon Army National Guard	$15.00
147th Fighter Wing, Texas Air National Guard	$15.00

Navy	Value
Admiral J.M. Boorda, Chief of Naval Operations	$20.00
Admiral Jay Johnson, Chief of Naval Operations	$20.00
John H. Dalton, Secretary	$25.00
USS Harry S. Truman CVN75	$15.00
USS Iwa Jima LHD-7 - Commissioned 2001	$25.00
USS Miami SSN755	$15.00
USS Saipan LHA-2	$15.00
Vice Admiral Kirk Donald	$20.00

SeeBee Chief
Commercial issue

Tun Tavern Marines
Commercial issue

USS Holland Proof Finish issue

COMMEMORATIVE MEDALS AND TOKENS

The collecting areas of tokens, commemorative medals and other ephemera, is very broad and exceptionally varied. Commemorative medals can center on an event or a person and will often express an opinion about this subject. Tokens are normally designed for a specific use, such as gaming or gambling, purchases with a specific business, or trade within an enclosed environment.

Medals produced in one country, but commemorating an event or person from another country, are usually considered less desirable than those with stronger geographic origins to the theme. For instance, an Osama Bin Laden medal produced in the U.S. would normally be less valuable than one designed and struck in Saudi Arabia or Afghanistan.

The selection of medals and tokens we have presented here are representative of both the types of items found in the Middle East and those available in the United States.

U.S. AIR FORCE PHOTO BY STAFF SGT. DERRICK C. GOODE

Value

Saddam Hussein portrait/Iraq map, ND(1968), **$15.00**
Social Revolution - July 1968, Hussein as President
- Supreme Commander of Iraq, Copper-nickel

2500th Anniversary of Iranian Empire, SH1350 **$25.00**
(1971), Kingdom of Iran, Silver, 30mm

Value

Camel with mihmal/Austria eagle, ND(1912), **$12.50**
Pilgrimage token/ Foreign Legion, Gold
washed copper, 40mm

Saddam Hussein National Literacy campaign, **$10.00**
AD1979-AH1400, Elimination of illiteracy,
Nickel clad steel, 33mm

Liberty Medal,
Commemorating 9-11

Medal of Congress, U.S. Mint, Unique, 1991, **$10,000.00**
General H. Norman Schwarzkopf, Gold, 3 inches

Medal of Congress, U.S. Mint, 1991, **$12.50**
General H. Norman Schwarzkopf, Bronze, 3 inches

	Value
Medal of Congress, U.S. Mint, 1991, General H. Norman Schwarzkop, Bronze, 1-1/2 inches	$3.50
Medal of Congress, U.S. Mint, Unique, 1991, Colin L. Powell, Gold, 3 inches	$10,000.00
Medal of Congress, U.S. Mint, 1991, Colin L. Powell, Bronze, 3 inches	$12.50
Medal of Congress, U.S. Mint, 1991, Colin L. Powell, Bronze, 1-1/2 inches	$3.50
Persian Gulf War, Commemorative Ounce, 1991, Set of Five designs, proof finish, Silver, 39mm	$55.00
Liberty Medal, ND, 9-11, Libert, Justice, Enduring Freedom, Brass, 34.5mm	$3.00

Value

Official U.S. Target/Saddam Hussein legacy, 2003, $5.00
Taking aim at Saddam Hussein, Copper- Nickel
plated copper, 27mm

Tokens

Wanted Dead or Alive/One Bin Laden, 2003, $5.00
Hunt for Osama Bin Laden, Brass, 27mm

Cie De Menthe De La Syrie, ND, Syrian amusement/ $4.00
Trade token good for one franc, Aluminum-bronze,
21mm

Value

Ramses Hilton Casino - Cairo, ND, Gaming token $3.00
from Egypt, Copper-Nickel, 27.5mm

Value

Casino Du Liban 50 P.L./Tree, ND, Gaming $6.50
token from Lebanon, Copper-nickel, 23mm

Sinbad's Dubai, ND, Gaming token from Dubai, $3.00
Copper-Nickel, 23mm

Sinbad's Dubai, ND,
Gaming token from Dubai

PAPER ITEMS

BOOKS

In the general retail trade, books about military conflicts come in two basic types. Memoirs or those that describe an insiders' view of the war and academic, or those which attempt to analyze or give historic perspective to events. Normally speaking memoirs tend to be the more desirable of these two types and are prized for their firsthand accounts of military life. Histories often give a more comprehensive overview however, and are sought by readers for their broad interpretations of interactions.

Unit histories and military manuals are two specific types of military books, not normally found in the retail trade. These are very data oriented by nature and therefore normally have smaller audiences. This does not mean, however, that they are of lesser value. While many military manuals can be obtained for minimal amounts, often between $3.00 and $10.00, Unit histories are usually quite expensive normally running in a range from $35.00 to $250.

In compiling this chapter we have concentrated on soldiers memoirs, imbedded journalist and photographers first-hand accounts and historic texts with a military lean. Government Printing Office volumes are well represented, as are the titles most often encountered in retail bookstores and on the Internet. All titles are grouped by conflict, with conflicts placed chronologically. Within the groupings, titles are arranged alphabetically. To round out this chapter we have included a small section of country specific histories for Middle East nations.

25th Infantry Division Soldiers, assigned to the Joint Logistics Command out of Bagram, Afghanistan, prepare a vehicle to be sling-loaded by a Chinook helicopter (CH-47). 25th ID Soldiers are deployed to Afghanistan in support of Operation Enduring Freedom.

A group of Area Handbooks published by the U.S. Government Printing Office between 1960 and 1977, covering countries of the Middle East. Each book in this U.S. Army series covered a specific country and offered in-depth information on all subjects pertaining to the area. Copies can be found in original tan card covers, official green hard covers and library rebound hard covers of various colors. Values average about $3 each for ex-library copies, but the information is very outdated.

	Value

Iran Hostage Crisis

	Value
America Held Hostage: The Iran Hostage Crisis and the I, Barbara Silberdick Feinberg and Don Lawson, Franklin Watts, 1991, HC	**$10.00**
Love From America, Alex Paen with James H. Brown, Roundtable Publishing, 1989, HC in DJ	**$12.50**
No Hiding Place - Inside Report on the Hostage Crisis, Robert D. McFadden, Joseph B Treaster and Maurice Carroll, Crown Publishing Group, 1981, HC in DJ	**$8.50**
October Surprise, Barbara Honegger, Tudor Publishers, 1989, HC in DJ	**$6.00**
October Surprise: America's Hostages in Iran and the Election of Ronald Reagan, Gary Sick, Times Books, 1992, HC in DJ	**$8.00**
Taken Hostage: The Iran Hostage Crisis and America's First Encounter with Radical Islam, David Farber, Princeton University Press, 2004, HC in DJ	**$12.00**
The Guts to Try - The Untold Story of the Iran Hostage Rescue Mission by the On-Scene Commander, Colonel James H. Kyle, USAF (Ret.) with John Robert Eidson, Orion Books, 1990, HC in DJ	**$7.50**

	Value
Twenty Years of Islamic Revolution: Political and Social Transition in Iran Since 1979, Eric J. Hooglund, Syracuse University Press, 2002, SC	**$14.50**
US Foreign Policy and the Iran Hostage Crisis, David Patrick Houghton, Cambridge University Press, 2001, SC	**$27.50**

Somalia Mission

	Value
Black Hawk Down, Mark Bowden, Pub Group West, 1999, HC in DJ	**$15.00**
In The Company of Heroes, Michael J. Durant with Steven Hartov, Putnam Publishing Group, 2003, HC in DJ	**$8.00**
Learning From Somolia, ed. Jeffrey Herbst and Walter Clarke, Westview Press, 1997, SC	**$45.00**
Losing Mogadishu - Testing U.S. Policy in Somalia, Jonathan Stevenson, Naval Institute Press, 1995, HC in DJ	**$16.50**
Somalia On $5 A Day: A Soldier's Story, Martin Stanton, Presidio Press, 2001, HC in DJ	**$10.00**
Somolia Operations: Lessons Learned, Kenneth Allard, University Press of the Pacific, 2002, SC	**$16.00**

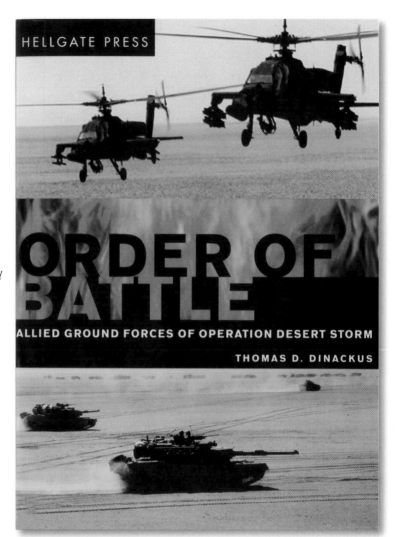

HELLGATE PRESS

ORDER OF BATTLE

ALLIED GROUND FORCES OF OPERATION DESERT STORM

THOMAS D. DINACKUS

Order of Battle by Thomas Dinackus, a complete reference of the Allied Ground Forces in Operation Desert Storm, $18.50.

	Value
Gulf War	
Airwar Over the Gulf, Eric Micheletti, Windrow and Greene, 1991, SC	$18.00
After Desert Storm: The United States Army and the Reconstruction of Kuwait, Government Printing Office, 1999, SC	$23.00
America's Splendid Little Wars: A Short History of U.S. Military Engagements: 1975-2000, Peter Huchthausen, Viking, 2003, HC in DJ	$10.00
Bombs Over Baghdad - Desert Storm for the Liberation of Kuwait - A Personal Narrative, Ron Weiss, Dorrance Publishing, 2001, SC	$12.50
Bravo Two Zero - The True Story of an SAS Patrol Behind the Lines in Iraq, Andy McNab, Bantam Press, 1993, HC in DJ	$25.00
Certain Victory: The United States Army in the Gulf War, Government Printing Office, 1993, HC	$191.00

	Value
Company C - The Real War in Iraq, John Sack, William Morrow, 1995, HC in DJ	$6.00
Conduct of the Persian Gulf Conflict: An Interim Report to Congress, 1991, Government Printing Office, 1991, SC	$25.00
Crusade: The Untold Story of the Persian Gulf War, Rick Atkinson, Houghton Mifflin, 1993, HC in DJ	$12.50
Decisive Force - Strategic Bombing In The Gulf War, Richard G. Davis, Air Force History Museum, 1996, SC	$10.00
Decisive Force: Strategic Bombing in the Gulf War, Government Printing Office, 1996, SC	$10.50
Decisive Force: Strategic Bombing in the Gulf War, Government Printing Office, 1996, SC	$10.50
Desert Fist - Allied Airpower for Desert Storm, Ian Black, Airlike Publishing Limited, 1991, SC	$7.50
Desert Storm: The Weapons of War, Eliot Brenner, William Harwood and the editors of the UPI, Orion Books, 1991, SC	$8.00

Three youth books which attempt to explain the complexities of several Middle East conflicts including the Persian Gulf War and the War in Iraq.

	Value		Value
Desert Warrior: A Personal View of the Gulf War by the Joint Forces Commander, HRH Gen. Khaled Bin Sultan with Patrick Seale, Harper Collins, 1995, HC in DJ	$8.00	From The Line in the Sand: Accounts of USAF Company Grade Officers in Support of Desert Shield/Desert Storm, Capt. Michael P. Vriesenga, Air University Press, 1994, SC	$12.50
Development of the Base Force, 1989-1992, Government Printing Office, 1993, SC	$7.00	Ground War Desert Storm, Jim Mesko, Squadron/Signal Publications, 1991, SC	$3.00
Encyclopedia of the Persian Gulf War, Richard Alan Schwartz, McFarland, 1998, HC	$45.00	Gulf Air War - Debreif - Described by the Pilots that Fought, ed. Stan Morse, Aerospace Publishing Limited, 1992, HC	$10.00
Falcon's Cry - A Desert Storm Memoir, Major Michael Donnelly and Denise Donnelly, Praeger Publishers, 1998, HC in DJ	$6.00	Gulf War Air Power Survey: Volume 1: Planning and Command and Control, Government Printing Office, 1993, SC	$56.50
Forty Days, Bob Simon, G.P. Putnam's Sons, 1992, HC	$7.00	Gulf War Air Power Survey: Volume 2: Operations and Effects and Effectiveness, Government Printing Office, 1993, SC	$62.00
From Shield to Storm: High Tech Weapons, Military Strategy & Coalition Warefare in the Persian Gulf, James Dunnigan and Austin Bay, William Morrow and Company, 1992, HC in DJ	$9.00	Gulf War Air Power Survey: Volume 3: Logistics and Support, Government Printing Office, 1993, SC	$60.00
From the Fulda Gap to Kuwait: United States Army, Europe, and the Gulf War, Government Printing Office, 1998, SC	$20.00	Gulf War Air Power Survey: Volume 4: Weapons, Tactics, and Training and Space Operations, Government Printing Office, 1993, SC	$42.00

Women, children and war are addressed in these two books aimed at giving an understanding of new aspects of modern conflict.

	Value		Value
Gulf War Air Power Survey: Volume 5: A Statistical Compendium and Chronology, Government Printing Office, 1993, SC	$71.50	Invasion Kuwait: An English Woman's Tale, Jehan S. Rajab, Palgrave Mcmillan, 1996, SC	$8.00
Heart of the Storm: The Genesis of the Air Campaign Against Iraq, Col. Richard T. Reynolds, Air University Press, 2001, SC	$3.50	Iron Soldiers: How America's 1st Armored Division Crushed Iraq's Elite Republican Guard, Tom Carhart, Pocket Books, 1994, SC	$10.00
Hotel Warriors - Covering the Gulf War, John J. Fialka, Woodrow Wilson Center Press, 1992, SC	$5.00	It Doesn't Take A Hero: The Autobiography of General H. Norman Schwarzkopf, Gen. H. Norman Schwarzkopf, Bantam Dell, 1992, HC in DJ	$3.00
In The Eye Of The Storm - Commanding The Desert Rats In The Gulf War, Major General Patrick Cordingley, Hodder & Stoughton, 1996, HC in DJ	$15.00	Jarhead: A Marine's Chronicle of the Gulf War, Anthony Swofford, Scribner, 2003, SC	$5.00
In The Eye of the Storm: The Life of General H. Norman Schwarzkopf, Claudio Gatti and Roger Cohen, Berkley, 1992, SC	$4.00	Legacy in the Sand: The United States Army Armament, Munitions and Chemical Command in Operations Desert Shield and Desert Storm, Government Printing Office, 1993, SC	$26.50
Into The Storm - A U.S. Marine in the Persian Gulf, Phillip Thompson, McFarland, 2001, SC	$30.00	Military Intelligence, Government Printing Office, 1998, SC	$45.00
Into The Storm: A Study in Command, Tom Clancy with Gen. Fred Franks Jr., G. P. Putnam's Sons, 1997, HC in DJ	$6.00	Military Intelligence Story: A Photographic History, Government Printing Office, 1998, SC	$21.00

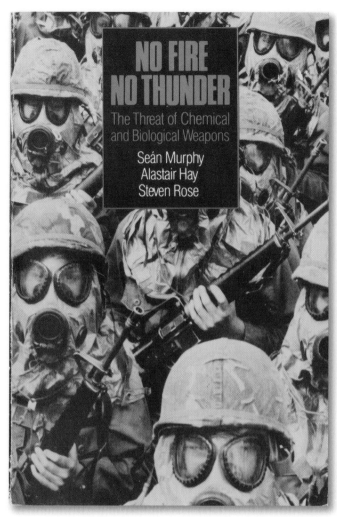

The threat of chemical and biological weapons has hung over the earth since World War I and has been an acute concern in Iraq, Iran and Afghanistan since the 1980's. Even with United Nations experts attempting to uncover and eliminate chemical and biological weapons research and production centers, military personnel must be prepared to protect themselves from the horrible consequences of these types of weapons. No Fire No Thunder – The Threat of Chemical and Biological Weapons attempted in 1984 to offer a better understanding of these types of weapons, scenarios of their use, consequences and methods of protection, $5.00.

	Value		Value
Military Lessons of the Gulf War, Bruce W. Watson, Greenhill Books, 1991, HC in DJ	$6.00	Operation Desert Shield: The First 90 Days, Eric Micheletti, Motorbooks International, 1990, SC	$12.50
Moving Mountains - Lessons in Leadership and Logistics from the Gulf War, Lt. Gen. William Pagones with Jeffrey Gruikshank, Harvard Business School Press, 1992, HC	$8.00	Order of Battle - Allied Ground Forces of Operation Desert Storm, Thomas D. Dinackus, Hellgate Press, 2000, SC	$18.50
My American Journey, General Colin L. Powell with Joseph E. Persico, Random House, 1995, HC in DJ	$7.50	Out of the Ashes - The Resurrection of Saddam Hussein, Andrew Cockburn and Patrick Cockburn, Harpercollins, 1999, HC in DJ	$7.00
No Fire No Thunder - The Threat of Chemical and Biological Weapons, Sean Murphy, Alastair Hay and Steven Rose, Monthly Review Press, 1984, SC	$5.00	Patterns of Global Terrorism, 2002, Government Printing Office, 2003, SC	$36.00
No Friends But The Mountains - The Tragic History of the Kurds, John Bulloch and Harvey Morris, Oxford University Press, 1992, HC in DJ	$15.00	Powerlift - Getting to desert Storm, Douglas Menarchik, Praeger, 1993, HC	$10.00
On Course to Desert Storm: The United States Navy and the Persian Gulf, Government Printing Office, 1992, SC	$19.00	Saddam Hussein and the Crisis in the Gulf, Judith Miller and Laurie Mylroie, Times Books, 1990, SC	$3.50
On Course to Desert Storm: The United States Navy and the Persian Gulf, Government Printing Office, 1992, SC	$19.00	Seeds Of Victory: Psychological Warfare and Propaganda, Richard D. Johnson, Schiffer Publishing, 1997, HC	$25.00
		Shield and Sword: The United States Navy and the Persian Gulf War, Government Printing Office, 1998, SC	$53.50

The Iranian hostage crisis was a turning point in our diplomatic and military involvement in the Middle East. When diplomacy failed we tried a military rescue raid to release the fifty-three hostages, but this too failed with the loss of eight lives. *The Guts to Try* by Colonel James H. Kyle, USAF (Ret.) presents an insiders view of what happened, $7.50.

	Value		Value
Shock and Awe: Achieving Rapid Dominance, Government Printing Office, 1996, SC	$26.00	The Desert Dogs Experience - Desert Storm and Desert Shield, Larry Gomoll, Private Printing, 1991, HC	$55.00
So Many, So Much, So Far, So Fast: United States Transportation Command and Strategic Deployment for Operation Desert Shield/Desert Storm, Government Printing Office, 1996, HC	$32.00	The Fire This Time: U.S. War Crimes in the Gulf, Ramsey Clark, Thunder's Mouth Press, 1992, HC in DJ	$6.00
Storm Command: A Personal Account of the Gulf War, General Sir Peter De La Billiere, Harper Collins, 1992, HC in DJ	$8.50	The G.I. Series - Gulf War Desert Shield and Desert Storm, 1990-1991, Anthony A. Evans, Greenhill Books/Stackpole Books, 2003, SC	$10.00
Strategic Implications of a Nuclear-Armed Iran, Government Printing Office, 2001, SC	$7.50	The Generals' War, Michael R. Gordon and General Bernard E. Trainor, Little, Brown and Company, 1995, SC	$4.00
Supporting the Troops: The United States Army Corps of Engineers in the Persian Gulf War, Government Printing Office, 1996, SC	$28.50	The Gulf Between Us - A Story of Love and Survival in Desert Storm, Cynthia B. Acree with Col. Cliff Acree, USMC, Brassey's, 2001, HC in DJ	$6.00
Swift and Effective Retribution: The United States Sixth Fleet and the Confrontation With Qaddafi, Government Printing Office, 1996, SC	$9.00	The Persian Gulf Crisis, Steve A. Yetiv, Greenwood Press, 1997, HC	$20.00
The Commanders, Bob Woodward, Simon & Schuster, 1991, HC in DJ	$8.00	This Ain't Hell... But You Can See It From Here! A Gulf War Sketchbook, Barry McWilliams, Presidio Press, 1992, SC	$6.50

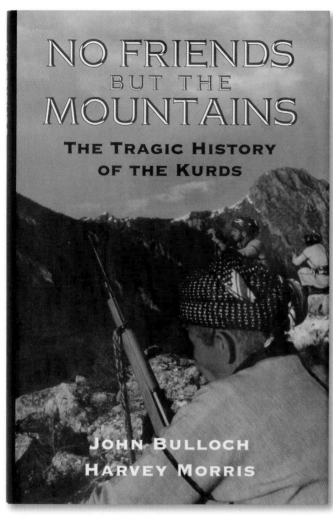

Near the close of the first Gulf War as our tanks approached the Euphrates River, President George H. Bush called for the people of Northern Iraq to rise up against Saddam Hussein. Kurdish guerrillas from the mountainous regions of the north did just that, but suffered dire consequences at the hands of the Iraqi military after the U.N. peace treaty was signed and U.S. military support was withdrawn. No Friends But The Mountains – The Tragic History of the Kurds, tells their story, $15.00.

	Value		Value
Thunder and Lightning: Vol. 1: Heart of the Storm, Col. Edward C. Mann III, Air University Press, 1995, SC	**$10.00**	U.S. Military Wheeled Vehicles, Michael Green and Greg Stewart, Concord Publications, 1993, SC	**$6.50**
Thunder and Lightning: Vol. 2: Desert Storm and Airpower Debates, Col. Edward C. Mann III, Air University Press, 1995, SC	**$8.00**	United States and the Persian Gulf: Reshaping Security Strategy for the Post-Containment Era, Government Printing Office, 2003, SC	**$15.00**
Triumph in The Desert: The Challenge, the Fighting, the Legacy, Peter David, Random House, 1991, HC in DJ	**$8.00**	United States Marines in the Persian Gulf, 1990-1991: Combat Service Support in Desert Shield and Desert Storm,, Government Printing Office, 1999, SC	**$29.50**
Triumph Without Victory - The Unreported History of the Persian Gulf War, Staff of U.S. News and World Report, Times Books, 1992, HC	**$5.00**	United States Marines in the Persian Gulf, 1990-1991: Humanitarian Operations in Northern Iraq, 1991: With Marines in Operation Provide Comfort, Government Printing Office, 1995, SC	**$18.00**
Twin Pillars to Desert Storm: America's Flawed Vision in the Middle East From Nixon to Bush, Howard Teicher, William Morrow & Co., 1993, HC in DJ	**$6.00**	United States Marines in the Persian Gulf, 1990-1991: Marine Communications in Desert Shield and Desert Storm, ,Government Printing Office, 1996, SC	**$19.00**
Tyranny's Ally - America's Failure to Defeat Saddam Hussein, David Wurmser, Aei Press, 1999, SC	**$7.00**	United States Marines in the Persian Gulf, 1990-1991: Third Marine Aircraft Wing in Desert Shield and Desert Storm, Government Printing Office, 1999, SC	**$25.00**
U.S. Forces in the Middle East, Anthony H. Cordesman, Westview Press, 1997, SC	**$8.00**		

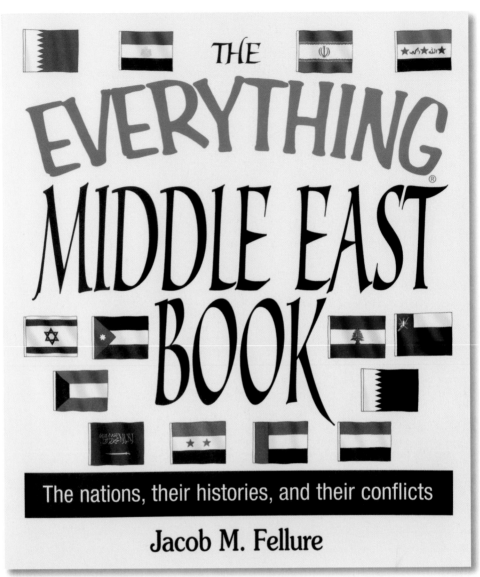

A great book to fill in the blanks in your general knowledge, The Everything Middle East Book covers the nations, their histories and their conflicts, $15.00.

	Value
United States Marines in the Persian Gulf, 1990-1991: With Marine Forces Afloat in Desert Shield and Desert Storm, Government Printing Office, 1998, SC	$29.50
Victory in the Gulf, Eric Micheletti and Yves Debay, Motorbooks International, 1991, SC	$8.00
Weapons of Desert Storm, ed. Walter J. Boyne, New Amerivan Library, 1991, SC	$5.00
Whirlwind War: The United States Army in Operations Desert Shield and Desert Storm, Government Printing Office, 1995, HC	$32.00

	Value
Afghanistan War	
Afghanistan Cave Complexes 1979-2004 - Mountain Stronholds of the Mujahideen, Taliban & Al Qaeda, Mir Bahmanyar and Ian Palmer, Osprey Pub. Co., 2004, SC	$18.00
Afghanistan The Bear Trap - The Defeat of a Superpower, Mohammad Yousaf and Mark Adkin, Casemate, 2001, HC in DJ	$8.00
Afghanistan: The Road to Kabul, Ron Haviv and Ilana Ozernoy, De.Mo, 2002, HC in DJ	$10.00

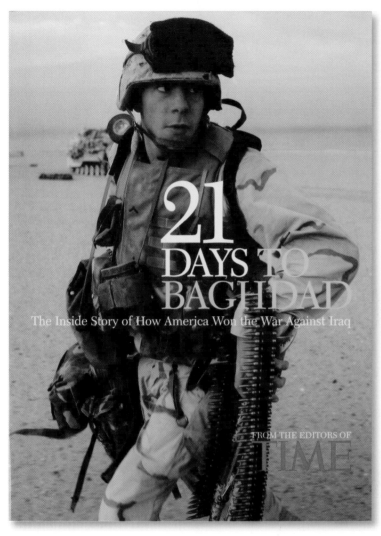

21 Days to Baghdad is one of the best photograph based books on the war in Iraq. Put together with eyewitness accounts from Time's imbedded correspondents it brings Operation Iraqi Freedom to the reader in full detail, value $12.50.

	Value		Value
Afghanistan - The Soviet Invasion and the Afghan Response, 1979-1982, M. Hassan Kakar, University of California Press, 1997, SC	$12.00	The Rise of the Taliban in Afghanistan: Mass Mobilization, Civil War, and the Future of the Region, Neamatollah Nojumi, Palgrave Macmillan, 2002, HC in DJ	$9.00
First In - An Insider's Account of How the CIA Spearheaded the War on Terror in Afghanistan, Gary C. Schroen, Presidio Press, 2005, HC in DJ	$14.00	Unfinished Business: Afghanistan, the Middle East and Beyond - Defusing The Dangers That Threaten America's Security, Harlan Ullman, Citadel Press, 2003, SC	$5.50

Iraq War

	Value		Value
Jihad! The Secret War in Afghanistan, Tom Carew, Trafalgar Square, 2001, HC in DJ	$9.00	A Fist in the Hornet's Nest: On the Ground in Baghdad Before During & After The War, Richard Engel, Hyperion Books, 2004, HC in DJ	$6.50
Not A Good Day To Die - The Untold Story of Operation Anaconda, Sean Naylor, Berkley, 2005, HC in DJ	$20.00	A Table in the Presence, Lt. Cary H. Cash, W. Publishing Group, 2004, HC in DJ	$8.00
Soldiers of God: With Islamic Warriors in Afghanistan and Pakistan, Robert D. Kaplan, Random House - Vintage Books, 2001, SC	$10.00	Airpower Against and Army: Challenge and Response in CENTAF's Duel With the Republican Guard, Lt. Col. William F. Andrews, Air University Press, 1998, SC	$10.00
Special Forces in Afghanistan 2001-2003: War Against Terrorism, Eric Micheletti, Historie & Collections, 2003, HC in DJ	$25.00		

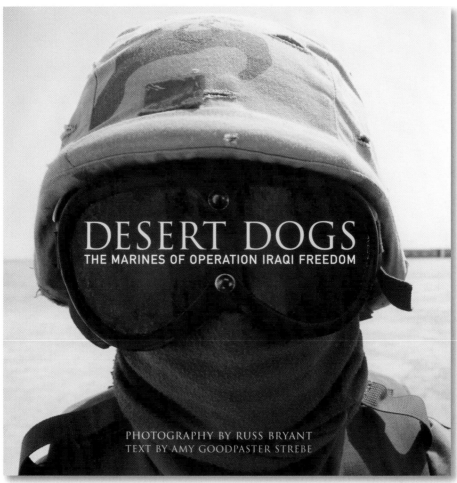

One very personal look at our current war in Iraq is offered through the pages of Desert Dogs – The Marines of Operation Iraqi Freedom. Using color pictures and brief text this book presents the average existence of a marine engaged in desert duty, value $14.00.

	Value		Value
Among Warriors in Iraq - True Grit, Special Ops, and the Raiding in Mosul and Fallujah, Mike Tucker, The Lyons Press, 2005, SC	$12.50	Disarming Iraq, Hans Blix, Pantheon Books, 2004, HC in DJ	$10.00
		Desert Dogs - The Marines of Operation Iraqi Freedom, Amy Goodpaster Strebe and Russ Bryant, Motorbooks International, 2004, SC	$14.00
Baghdad Bulletin: The Real Story of the War in Iraq - Reporting From Beyond The Green Zone, David Enders, University of Michigan Press, 2005, HC in DJ	$17.50	Genration Kill: Devil Dogs, Iceman, Captain America, and the New Face of American War, Evan Wright, Putnam Publishing Group, 2004, HC in DJ	$16.50
Blinded by the Sunlight - Emerging From the Prison of Saddam's Iraq, Matthew McAllester, Harpercollins, 2004, HC in DJ	$10.00	Heavy Metal - A Tank Company's Battle To Baghdad, Capt. Jason Conroy with Ron Martz, Potomac Books, 2005, HC	$18.00
Boots On The Ground - A Month with the 82nd Airbourne In The Battle For Iraq, Karl Zinsmeister, Truman Talley Books, 2003, HC in DJ	$16.50	In The Company of Soldiers - A Chronicle of Combat, Rick Atkinson, Henry Holt & Co., 2004, HC in DJ	$8.00
Conflict Iraq: Weapons and Tactics of the US and Iraqi Forces, David Miller, Zenith Press, 2003, SC	$9.00	Live From Bagdad, Robert Weiner, Doubleday, 1992, HC in DJ	$7.00
Dawn Over Baghdad: How The U.S. Military Is Using Bullets and Ballots to Remake Iraq, Karl Zinsmeister, Encounter Books, 2004, HC in DJ	$6.00	Martyrs: Innocence, Vengeance, and Despair in the Middle East, Joyce M. Davis, Palgrave Macmillan, 2004, SC	$7.00
		McCoy's Marines - Darkside to Baghdad, John Koopman, Zenith Press, 2005, HC in DJ	$18.00

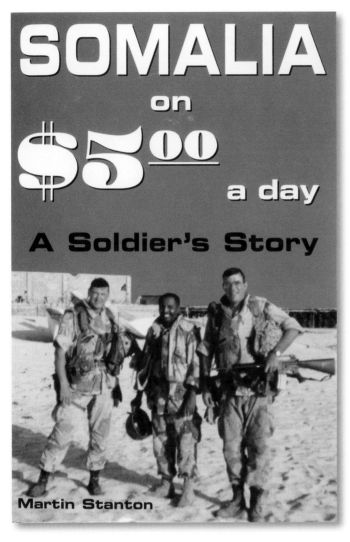

SOMALIA
on
$5.00
a day

A Soldier's Story

Martin Stanton

Somalia on $5 A Day is one of the most recognized and respected active duty military memoirs published in current times. It provides a real glimpse of the practical applications on the ground of the U.S.'s politically based peace keeping missions abroad. The $5 a day is simply a breakdown of the $150 a month imminent danger or combat pay a soldier receives when they are sent to serve in a hostile fire or war zone, value $10.00.

	Value
Naked in Baghdad: The Iraq War As Seen By NPR's Correspondent, Anne Garrels, Farrar, Straus & Giroux, 2003, HC in DJ	$6.00
Operation Iraqi Freedom - 22 Historic Days in Words and Pictures, Marc Kusnetz, William M. Arkin, Gen. Montgomery Meigs ret. And Neil Shapiro, Andrews McMeel Publishing, 2003, HC in DJ	$15.00
Saddam: King of Terror, Con Coughlin, Ecco Press, 2002, HC in DJ	$8.00
Saddam's Secrets: The Hunt for Iraq's Hidden Weapons, Tim Trevan, HarperCollins, 1999, SC	$5.00
Shooter - The Autobiography of the Top-Ranked Marine Sniper, Gunnery Sgt. Jack Coughlin and Capt. Casey Huhlman with Donald A Davis, St. Martin's Press, 2005, HC in DJ	$20.00
Sister in the Band of Brother: Embedded with the 101st Airborne in Iraq, Katherine M. Skiba, University Press of Kansas, 2005, SC	$12.00

	Value
Spare Parts: A Marine Reservist's Journey from Campus to Combat in 38 Days, Buzz Williams, Gotham Books, 2004, HC	$6.00
Special Operations in Iraq, Mike Ryan, Pen & Sword Books, 2004, HC in DJ	$35.00
The Freedom:Shadows and Hallucinations in Occupied Iraq, Christian Parenti and Teru Kuwayama, New Press, 2004, HC in DJ	$15.00
The Gift of Valor - A War Story, Michael M. Phillips, Broadway Books, 2005, HC in DJ	$7.00
The Iraq War, John Keegan, Alfred A. Knopf, 2004, HC in DJ	$12.50
The Iraq War - A Military History, Williamson Murray and Major Gen. Robert H. Scales Jr., Belknap Press, 2003, HC in DJ	$10.00
The Iraq War - As Witnessed by the Correspondents and Photographers of United Press International, ed. Martin Walker, Brassey's, 2004, SC	$7.50

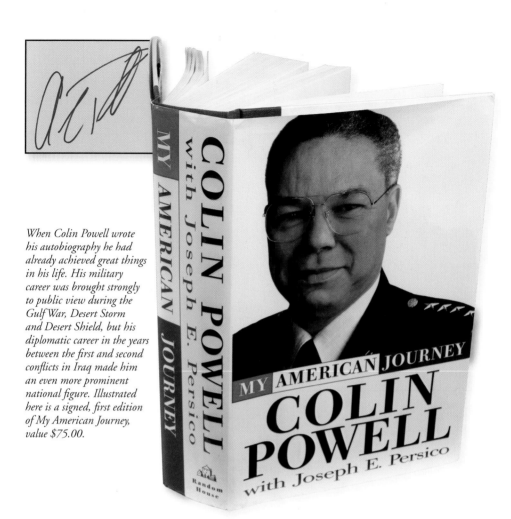

When Colin Powell wrote his autobiography he had already achieved great things in his life. His military career was brought strongly to public view during the Gulf War, Desert Storm and Desert Shield, but his diplomatic career in the years between the first and second conflicts in Iraq made him an even more prominent national figure. Illustrated here is a signed, first edition of My American Journey, value $75.00.

	Value
The March Up: Taking Baghdad with the 1st Marine Division, Ray L Smith and Bing West, Bantam, 2003, HC in DJ	$18.00
The Path to Victory: America's Army and the Revolution in Human Affairs, Donald Vandergriff, Presidio Press, 2002, HC in DJ	$12.00
The War In Iraq, , Regan Books, 2003, SC	$15.00
The War in Iraq - The Illustrated History, the Editors of One Nation (Life magazine), Time Inc, 2003, HC in DJ	$12.50
This Man's Army - A Soldier's Story from the Front Lines of the War on Terrorism, Andrew Exum, Gotham Books, 2004, HC in DJ	$16.00
Thunder Run: The Armored Strike to Capture Baghdad, Mark Bowden, Atlantic Monthly Press, 2004, HC in DJ	$17.50
21 Days to Baghdad - The Inside Story of How America Won the War Against Iraq, editors of Time magazine, Time Inc, 2003, HC in DJ	$12.50
Winning Modern Wars: Iraq, Terrorism, and the American Empire, Wesley K. Clark, Perseus Books Group, 2003, HC in DJ	$5.00

	Value
Witness Iraq: A War Journal, February - April 2003, ed. Marcel Saba, PowerHouse Books, 2003, HC	$10.00

Middle East

	Value
A History of Modern Palestine: One Land, Two Peoples, Ilan Pappe, Cambridge University Press, 2003, HC	$35.00
A History of Modern Yemen, Paul Dresch, Cambridge University Press, 2001, SC	$17.50
A History of Saudi Arabia, Madawi Al-Rasheed, Cambridge University Press, 2002, SC	$10.00
A Portrait of Egypt: A Journey Through the World of Militant Islam, Mary Anne Weaver, Farrar, Straus and Giroux, 1998, HC in DJ	$10.00
Egypt at the Crossroads: Domestic Stability and Regional Role, Government Printing Office, 1999, SC	$20.00
Elite Forces of India and Pakistan, Ken Conboy and Paul Hannon, Osprey Publishing, 1992, SC	$15.00
Foreign Country Studies: Ethiopia, Government Printing Office, 1993, SC	$37.50

A Time Books Special Report from 1990, Saddam Hussein and the Crisis in the Gulf, one of many paperbacks produced after the Iraqi invasion of Kuwait, value $3.50.

	Value
Foreign Country Studies: Jordan, Government Printing Office, 1991, SC	**$31.00**
Foreign Country Studies: Lebanon, Government Printing Office, 1989, SC	**$28.00**
Foreign Country Studies: Pakistan, Government Printing Office, 1995, SC	**$31.00**
Foreign Country Studies: Somalia, Government Printing Office, 1993, SC	**$31.00**
Foreign Country Studies: Sudan, Government Printing Office, 1992, SC	**$34.00**
Foreign Country Studies: Turkey, Government Printing Office, 1995, SC	**$34.00**
From Trucial States to United Arab Emirates, Frauke Heard-Bey, Longman Group, 1981, HC in DJ	**$50.00**
Instability and Conflict in the Middle East: People, Petroleum and Security Threats, Naji Abi- Aad, Michel Grenon, Palgrave Macmillan, 1997, HC	**$40.00**
Iraq - Old Land, New nation in Conflict, William Spencer, Twenty First Century Books, 2000, HC in DJ	**$8.00**

	Value
Israel and the Arabs, Ahron Bregman and Jihan El-Tahri, TV Books, 2000, SC	**$6.00**
Pakistan: In the Shadow of Jihad and Afghanistan, Mary Anne Weaver, Farrar, Straus and Giroux, 2002, HC in DJ	**$7.00**
The Arab-Israeli Wars, Chaim Herzog, Randon House, 1984, SC	**$8.00**
The Complete Idiot's Guide to Middle East Conflict, Mitchell Bard, Alpha Books, 2002, SC	**$12.50**
The Everything Middle East Book: The Nations, Their Histories and Their Conflicts, Jacob M. Fellure, Adams Media, 2004, SC	**$15.00**
United Arab Emirates Yearbook, Ibrahim Abed, Trident Press Ltd., 2002, HC	**$15.00**
War Without End: Israelis, Palestinians, and the Struggle for a Promised Land, Anton La Guardia, Thomas Dunne Books, 2002, HC in DJ	**$10.00**

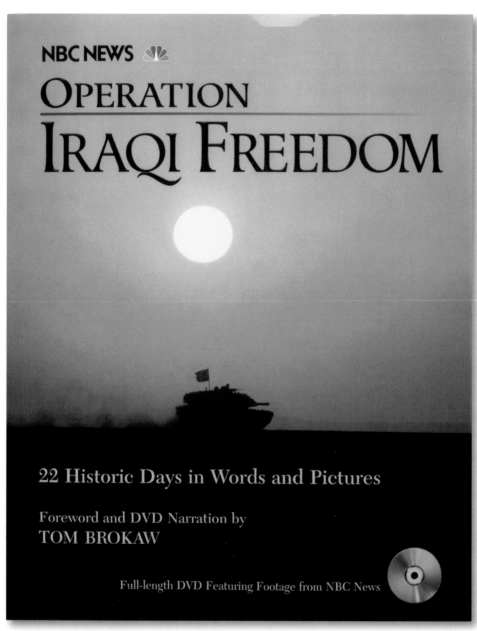

NBC NEWS

OPERATION
IRAQI FREEDOM

22 Historic Days in Words and Pictures

Foreword and DVD Narration by
TOM BROKAW

Full-length DVD Featuring Footage from NBC News

As a bonus feature, this NBC News book on Operation Iraqi Freedom is accompanied by a DVD with NBC News coverage of the war. value $15.00.

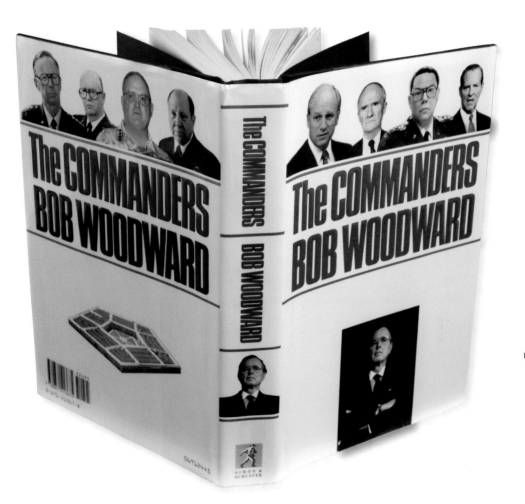

Bob Woodward's investigative journalism was turned on the military hierarchy and the new aggressive foreign policy for this Gulf War era analysis of *The Commanders*. Pictured on the dust jacket are: George Bush, Dick Cheney, Colin Powell, Norman Schwarzkopf, James Baker, Maxwell Thurmond, Brent Scowcroft, Thomas Kelly and William Crowe, $8.00.

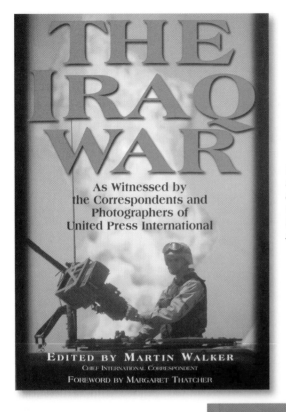

United Press International compiled this handy book of articles filed by their correspondents before, during and after the war in Iraq. This is primarily a text-based book, but the color photo section contains some very poignant images. value $7.50.

Volume 26 in the Fortress series from Osprey Publishing, an extensive examination of the Mountain Caves of the Taliban and Al Qaeda, contains photographs, diagrams and text. This reference does a good job of explaining the caves, their military uses and our troops difficulties in entering and clearing them. value $18.00.

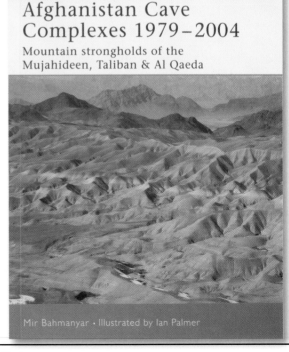

COMIC BOOKS

Wherever United States service personnel have traveled in the world, comic books have followed. That package of brief text and entertaining artwork has provided the necessary break from the tension and imminent dangers of war for soldiers from WWII to the War in Iraq. Compact yet colorful, complex but quick, comics are there when you need them and easy to stow for the soldier on the go.

Remembrances of Desert Storm provided the impetus for several individual comics as well as a fine series entitled *Desert Storm Journal*. Though we are certain that there were many different types and genres of comic books being read by our troops during the various Middle East conflicts from 1979 to today, we have chosen to list and illustrate in this chapter only those that deal with stories of these wars.

	Value		Value
Daffy Qaddafi: Malice in Wonderland, #1, Comics Unlimited, 1986	$2.00	Desert Storm Journal, Apple Comics, #8, December 1992	$2.50
Desert Storm Journal, Apple Comics, #1, Hussein cover, September 1991	$2.75	Desert Storm: Send Hussein To Hell, #1, Innovation, 1991	$2.00
Desert Storm Journal, Apple Comics, #1, Schwartzkopf cover, September 1991	$2.75	Dictators of the Twentieth Century: Saddam Hussein - The Rise, Antarctic Press, #1, August 2004	$5.00
Desert Storm Journal, Apple Comics, #2, December 1991	$2.50	Dictators of the Twentieth Century: Saddam Hussein - The Fall, Antarctic Press, #2, September 2004	$5.00
Desert Storm Journal, Apple Comics, #3, February 1992	$2.50	Reagan's Raiders, #1, Solson Publications, 1986	$2.00
Desert Storm Journal, Apple Comics, #4, April 1992	$2.50	Reagan's Raiders, #2, Solson Publications, 1986	$2.00
Desert Storm Journal, Apple Comics, #5, June 1992	$2.50	Reagan's Raiders, #3, Solson Publications, 1987	$2.00
Desert Storm Journal, Apple Comics, #6, August 1992	$2.50	The Story of Operation Desert Storm, #1 NEC, August 2003	$4.00
Desert Storm Journal, Apple Comics, #7, October 1992	$2.50	To Afghanistan and Back - A Graphic Travelogue by Ted Rall, HC in DJ, NBM, 2002	$16.00

Daffy Qaddafi: Malice in Wonderland, #1, Comics Unlimited, 1986

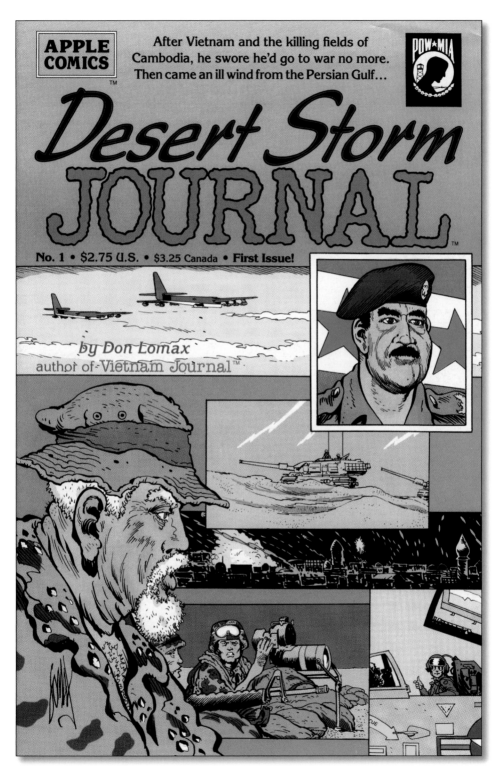

Desert Storm Journal, #1 (Hussein cover), Apple Comics, September 1991

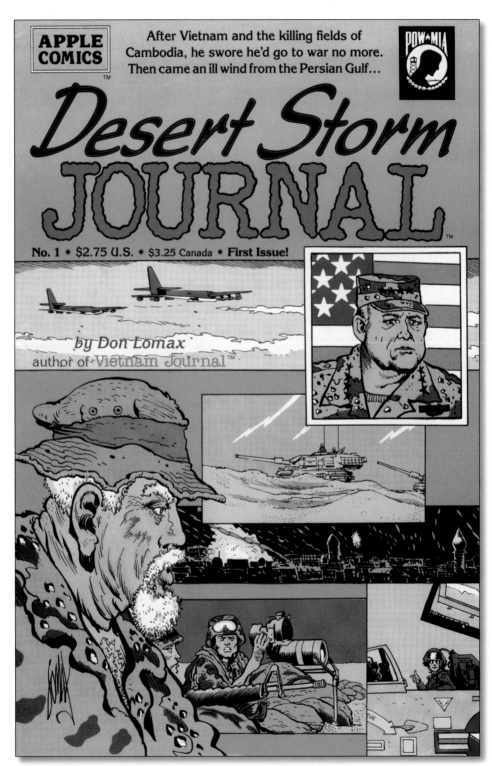

Desert Storm Journal, #1 (Schwartzkopt cover), Apple Comics, September 1991

Desert Storm Journal, #2, Apple Comics, December 1991

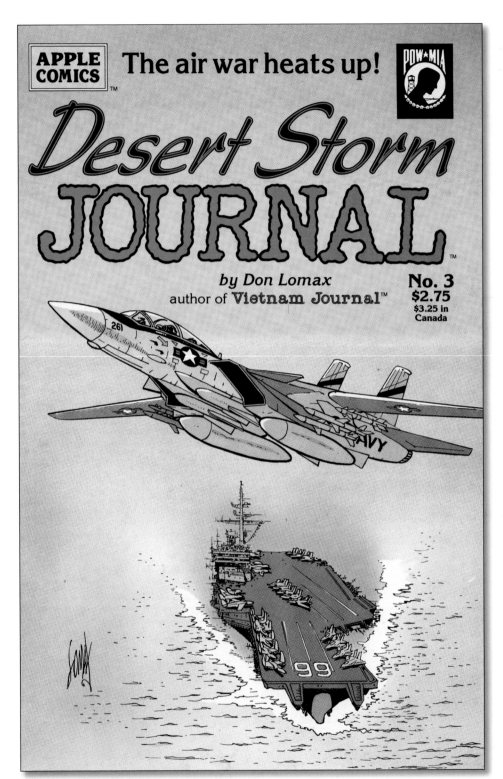

Desert Storm Journal, #3, Apple Comics, February 1992

Desert Storm Journal, #4, Apple Comics, April 1992

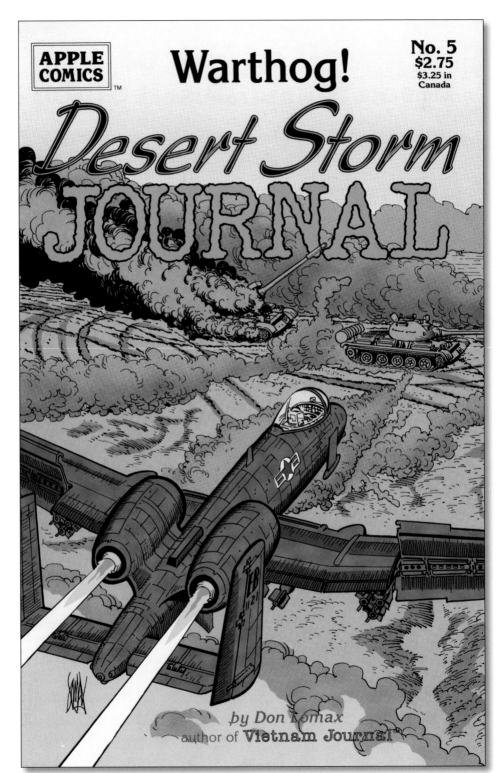

Desert Storm Journal, #5, Apple Comics, June 1992

Desert Storm Journal, #6, Apple Comics, August 1992

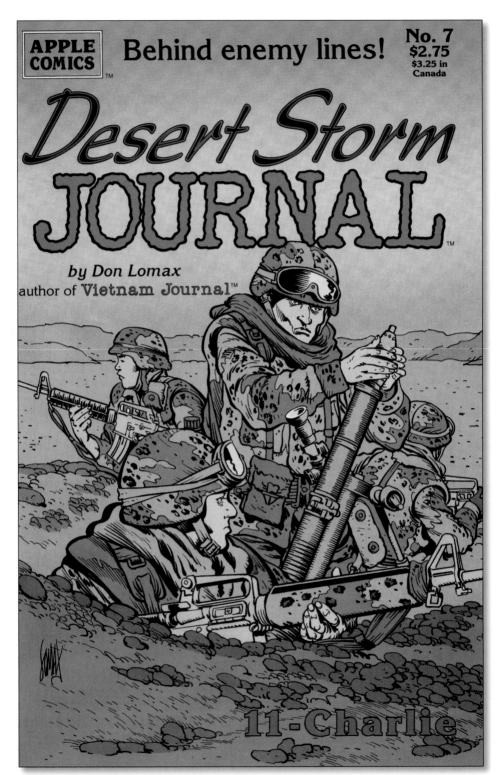

Desert Storm Journal, #7, Apple Comics, October 1992

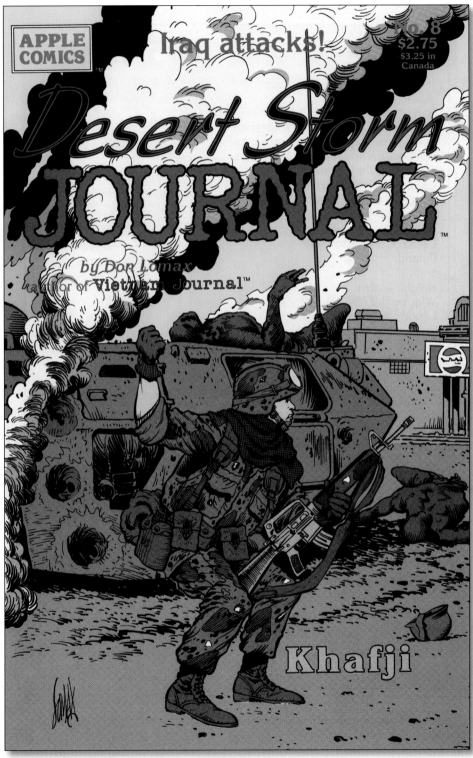

Desert Storm Journal, #8, Apple Comics, December 1992

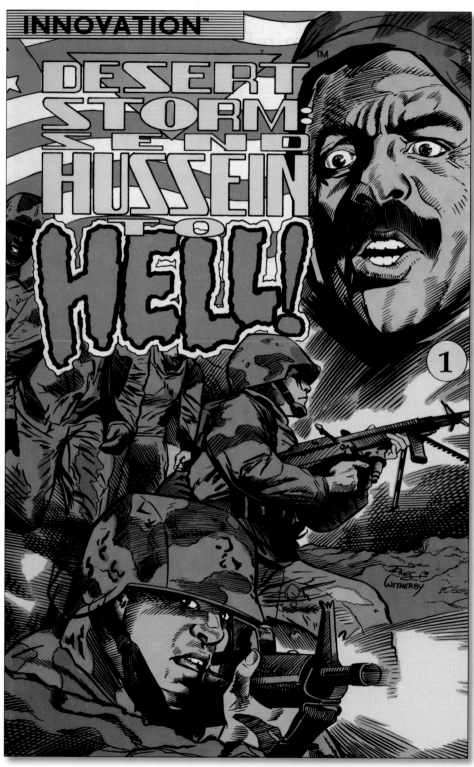

Desert Storm: Send Hussein To Hell, Innovation, 1991

The Story of Operation Desert Storm, #1, NEC, August 2003

To Afghanistan and Back - A Graphic Travelogue by Ted Rall, NBM, 2002

PROPAGANDA LEAFLETS

The use of propaganda in military operations probably dates back to the first major conflicts of mankind. The principles of getting to know ones enemy and using this knowledge against them in confrontations is elemental. Call it getting under their skin, psyching out an opponent, dissolving moral, getting inside your enemies head or spinning the situation. Anyway you define it, the methods are just about the same and the military PSYOP (Psychological Operations) units of today have worked these approaches down to a fine art.

Propaganda messages are delivered in many forms. Leaflets, posters, bumper stickers, imitation currency, video and audio tapes, loudspeakers, conversation, movies, TV and radio are all workable forms for the conveyance of propaganda.

Propaganda leaflets are probably the most versatile of all methods of conveyance. They are light and small, can be easily dropped from aircraft or handed out in person, and can present several types of messages. Some leaflets attempt to persuade the opposition of a singular point of view, while others simply present the actual facts or history of a situation in hopes that the reader will see the light. Other leaflets present implicit instructions, as in the example of safe conduct passes, or law

and order occupation issues. Each of these approaches is used for different situations and all can be extremely effective in achieving their goal.

All elements of leaflet production are equally important. The art and writing go hand in hand to fully convey the message and emotional subtexts desired by the issuer. Printing and distribution must be fast and efficient and able to adapt to situational variants. Language translation and cultural

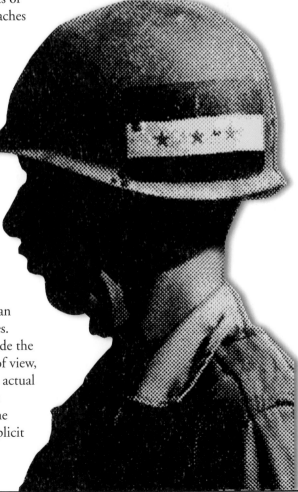

On May 4, 2004, an Afghan teacher discuss with First Sergeant Dale Perez the different topics taught to students in Gulbahar, Afghanistan. The Parwan Provincial Reconstruction Team donated toys, clothes, and school supplies on behalf of a church in the United States to the Gulbahar High School and Orphanage in Afghanistan.

differences must be carefully examined to avoid any misconceptions in the theme or message of the leaflet. All these functions must work together to produce a strong piece of propaganda and avoid the possibility of dismissal by the recipient.

Thought many propaganda leaflets are first produced as full color masters, the majority of those distributed during modern Middle east conflicts, have been printed in black and white. In the case of multinational or coalition allied conflicts there may be many PSYOP units working independently or together to produce the required materials. Confusion can sometimes be a side benefit of this arrangement, but over

production can lead to a situation such as was reported during the Iraq War, where in April 2003 imbedded news sources wrote that there were so many leaflets around that service personnel were gathering them for collections or other uses all the way down to toilet paper substitute.

Most of the following notes were disseminated during the Gulf War, when the use of propaganda leaflets was at a very high priority. Additional information, as well as buying and selling opportunities, for propaganda leaflets and other military propaganda materials is plentiful on the Internet. Recommended web sites include: www.psywarrior.com, www.psywar.org, and

A pair of propaganda notes from the current war in Iraq. One mimics the Iraqi banknotes in circulation when the invasion began. The other warns that bombs are going to be dropped and notes, **"Why are bombs dropping on you? Because of Saddam!"** *Propaganda notes are used to encourage the enemy to surrender, give up vital information, set down their weapons or otherwise abandon resistance, as well as to warn civilians to take cover indoors. value $3.00.*

٣٠

شباط

١٩٩١

كهانة صدام :
يجب ان تطمئنوا بانني سوف احل
مشكلة الكويت حتى تاريخ ٣٠
شباط ...

A three-panel cartoon of a scimitar swinging Saddam graces this Gulf War leaflet. This cartoon was drawn by Tim Wallace primarily for internal use of the command. Note the English language **"oops"** and **"thud"**. The backside translates as **"30 February 1991, Saddam's prediction: Be assured that I will solve the problem of Kuwait on 30 February…"** which is a joke only to those whose calendar does note contain that date! When this not was passed to a group in Turkey, they took it as a true propaganda note, printed it up and dropped it over Northern Iraq, even though it was never meant for distribution to a Middle East Audience. value $3.00.

*There are several varieties of the "Bomb" propaganda notes used in Iraq. The Bomb side normally says something like: **Warning! This is only the beginning! This could have been a real bomb. We desire the protection of innocent people and Saddam is leading them into certain death and destruction. We want you to know the truth! Saddam is the cause. Yes, the Multi-national Forces have the ability to launch a lightning attack anywhere at anytime. Warning!"** The pure text side of these notes each differ a bit, but the point usually is to make it clear that Saddam is the problem, and that there is no way for the Iraqi military to succeed against the overwhelming air superiority of the multinational forces. value $3.00.*

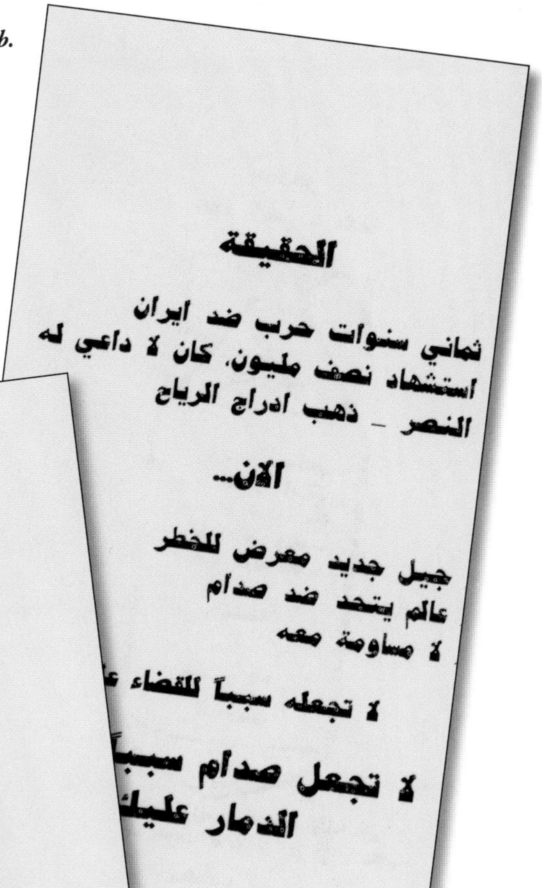

الحقيقة

ثماني سنوات حرب ضد ايران
استشهاد نصف مليون، كان لا داعي له
النصر ـ ذهب ادراج الرياح

الآن...

جيل جديد معرض للخطر
عالم يتحد ضد صدام
لا مساومة معه

لا تجعله سببا للقضاء ع

لا تجعل صدام سبب
الدمار عليك

تحذير!
هذه البداية هنا!

نمنى ان
تكون هذه
قنبلة حقيقية

نرغب في المحافظة
على الناس الابرياء
وصدام يقودهم في
طريق الدمار والموت
المحتوم. نريد اعلامهم

بالحقيقة!

صدام هو
السبب

نعم إن القوات المتعددة الجنسيات ل
قدرة على شن هجوم صاعق في اي آن او كان!
تحذير!

Pictured here is another version of the "Bomb" leaflet used in Iraq during the Gulf War. The bomb side again presents a stern warning and blames Saddam for the destruction to come. The back emphasizes, *"Resistance is purposeless. The outcome is inevitable. Save Yourselves. Leave your weapons and go immediately to a safe area."* value $3.00.

سياسة

صدام حسين

العدوانية تجاه الاوطان المجاورة

هي

السبب الوحيد

لتدمير العراق و استهدفت

المواقع العسكرية فقط.

يقع اللوم ألا على

صدام!

تحذير!
هذه البداية فقط!

نعسى ان
تكون هذه
قنبلة حقيقية

نرغب في المحافظة
على الاناس الابرياء
وصدام يقودهم في
طريق الدمار والموت
المحتوم نريد اعلامهم

بالحقيقة!

صدام هو
السبب

نعم. إن القوات المتعددة الجنسيات على
قدرة تامة بشن هجوم صاعق في اي ان او مكان!

تحذير!

يـاأبـناء الـعراق
بـالـمـوت تـطـيـل عـمـر صـدام ،
لـكـك تـقـصـر مـن عـمـر وطـنـك الـعراق

الـوَجْـهُ الـبَـارِدُ لِـلـمَـوْتِ والـحَـرْبْ

Pictured here is a stark Gulf War leaflet bearing Saddam Hussein's portrait and the legend, "**The Cold Face of Death In War**". The text on the reverse reads "**O' Sons of Iraq, In Death you lengthen the life of Saddam, but you shorten the life of your homeland, Iraq**". *value $5.00.*

*This Gulf War leaflet was designed to emphasize Saddam's disregard for human life and ugly habit of risking innocent civilians to shield military targets. The idea of this note is to illustrate that Saddam wants war and does not care about the amount of bloodshed. Front text surrounding Saddam reads, **"Saddam is the sole reason for the bombing of Iraq!"** The back side translates roughly as **"Saddam's aggression is the reason the whole world is at war with Iraq. The Coalition Air Forces are trying their bests to avoid injuring innocent civilians. But Saddam has placed Iraqi civilians within military areas to die instead of his loyal military personnel. He is ready to sacrifice all of you, the holy places as well as the history of Iraq for his own survival."** value $4.00.*

إن حكم صدام الظالم يحتضر فقد أوشك على النهاية.

يقف العديد من موالي صدام مع قوات الإئتلاف. ولقد إختارت وحدات العراق العسكرية عدم القتال من أجل صدام. فالجنود يلقون أسلحتهم ويتركون معسكراتهم للرجوع إلى عائلاتهم.

قريبا، سيتحرر شعب العراق من نظام صدام الغاشم.

يفقد صدام دعم قواته العسكرية.

One of the many leaflets used during Operation Iraqi Freedom. This particular type would have been first used in April 2003 as Coalition forces advanced on Baghdad and Basra. The front of the leaflet depicts Iraqi soldiers as well as abandoned equipment and reads: **"Saddam is losing support of his military forces".** *The back is all text within an intricate border. A rough translation would be:* **"Saddam's oppressive rule is coming to an end. Many of Saddam's supporters are siding with Coalition forces. Iraq's military units are choosing not to fight for Saddam. Soldiers are laying down their weapons and leaving their posts to return to their families. Shortly the people of Iraq will be free from his brutal regime".** *value $6.00.*

*Pictured here is another variety of the Iraqi 25 Dinar banknote. This version bears the large question mark on the back and asserts that **Coalition forces are well fed and the reader of this note could be also, since prisoners of war are fed the same as soldiers on the Coalition side.** value $3.00.*

The type of childish color cartoon drawing seen on this propaganda leaflet was meant to invoke a feeling of childlike innocence, sincerity and longing for family. The message is basic, **die fighting against superior forces, or live in the loving arms of your family.** The backside of this leaflet displays flags from the various Coalition nations. value $4.00.

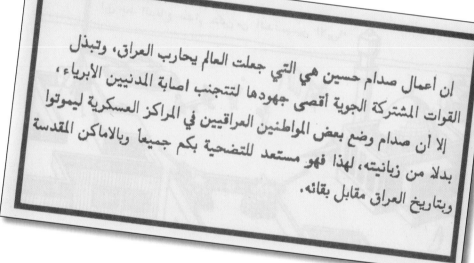

The Coalition used propaganda leaflets to expose Saddam's practice of using civilian areas to house military equipment. On this note we see children and Mosques at risk because of this repulsive policy. On the back of this note we are told that **Saddam has brought this war to Iraq and that civilian deaths are on his head.** *value $4.00.*

إلقاء النفط وتسريبه عمدا يسمم الممرات المائية العراقية،

كما إنه يفسد أيضا مستقبل عائلاتكم.

IZ D046

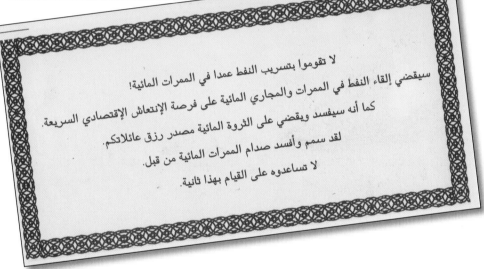

لا تقوموا بتسريب النفط عمدا في الممرات المائية!

سيقضي إلقاء النفط في الممرات والمجاري المائية على فرصة الإنتعاش الإقتصادي السريع.

كما أنه سيفسد ويقضي على الثروة المائية مصدر رزق عائلاتكم.

لقد سمم وأفسد صدام الممرات المائية من قبل.

لا تساعدوه على القيام بهذا ثانية.

During the Gulf War purposeful oil spills caused much damage to the environment. This leaflet was designed to combat a recurrence of this problem during the War in Iraq. The front shows a family of Iraqi civilians and notes **"Dumping oil poisons Iraqi waterways, as well as your family's future".** *The back warns that dumping oil and tainting sea life will impede economic recovery after the war. value $8.00.*

MEMORABILIA

DESERT STORM
F-4G PHANTOM "WILD WEASEL"

Limited
Collector's
Edition

7

THE F-4G PHANT
EXPOSE AND D
THE WILD WE
RADAR EMITTE
HARM OR AGM-
SPEED ANTIRA
KEY TO SUCCE
ATTACKING "FO
TERRITORY UND

SI

WINGSPAN . . . . .
LENGTH . . . . . .
HEIGHT . . . . . .
WEIGHT (MAX
MAXIMUM SPE
MAXIMUM RAN
SERVICE CEIL

F-4G PHANTOM "WILD WEAS

افأة

٢٥ مليون دولار اميركي

٩٦٤٨

tips@orha.centcom.m

PERSONAL MEMENTOS

People collect many different things and we all collect for unique reasons. For many generations our troops serving overseas have brought back interesting trinkets, artifacts and memorabilia from their journeys and in turn those of us who stayed home have collected items which remind us of our loved ones who are away.

Sometimes it's a picture or piece of correspondence, which hold the most significant meaning. In other instances we most fondly remember items bought in markets, picked up in the street or even given in thanks for service and friendship. They may be of limited collector value, or worth significant amounts, but most importantly they have meaning to us.

As we compiled the other chapters in this book, on coins, paper money and related items from the Middle East conflicts we came across several items that did not fit into our basic chapters, but which held our interest. To round out this book and to give you a glimpse of the wide breadth of modern memorabilia brought back from the Middle East or acquired here in the United States we offer this catch all chapter.

Private First Class Michael Player, Task Force 1-63 Armor, writes notes in the sleeping quarters in a safe house in the Northern Iraqi city of Byhassan during Operation Iraqi Freedom on Dec. 7, 2003. Operation Iraqi Freedom is a multi-national coalition effort to liberate the Iraqi people, eliminate Iraq's weapons of mass destruction and end the regime of Saddam Hussein.

USS Theodore Roosevelt cap with Naval rating pin back and large patch.

United States Navy – Line of Death patch

Coca-Cola bottle in Arabic along side Coca-Cola bottle in Hebrew

Front

Back

American Legion — Supports Our Troops, yellow ribbon and flag tee shirt. One of many items sold in the U.S. displaying the ribbon of support for those who serve.

A black and white patterned Kaffiyeh head covering held in place by the black-corded ekal.

Corded necklace with pendant displaying an English name in Arabic. This example belongs to Kevin, who was kind enough to lend it to us for photography.

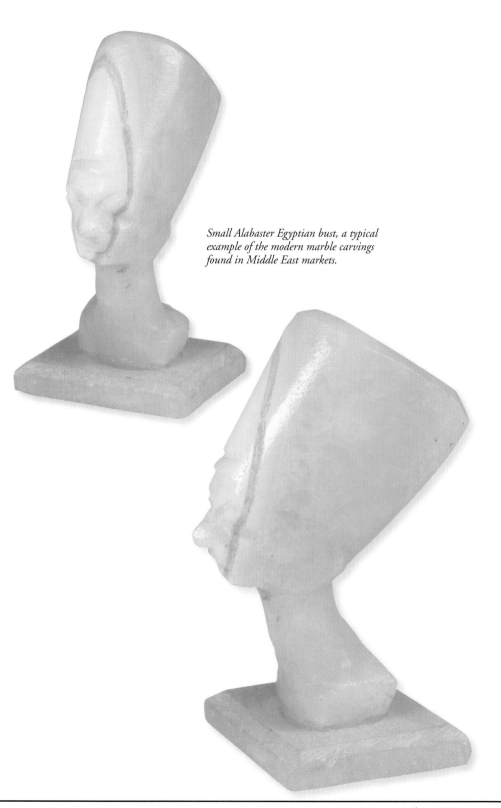

Small Alabaster Egyptian bust, a typical example of the modern marble carvings found in Middle East markets.

Current magazines with cover photos from the War in Iraq.
Informative now, historical collectibles in the future.

A selection of current Time magazines covering the War in Afghanistan and the War in Iraq. Many of Time's covers feature American soldiers in service of their country.

U.S. $50 Series EE Patriot Bond, costs $25 and is guaranteed to double in value over a 20-year period. Can be cashed in after 5 years without penalty and pays interest for up to 30-years.

U.S. $75 Series EE Patriot Bond, costs $37.50 and is guaranteed to double in value over a 20-year period. Can be cashed in after 5 years without penalty and pays interest for up to 30-years.

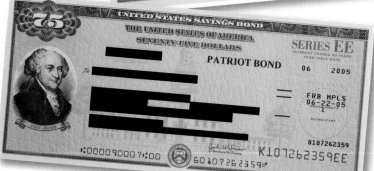

U.S. $100 Series EE Patriot Bond, costs $50 and is guaranteed to double in value over a 20-year period. Can be cashed in after 5 years without penalty and pays interest for up to 30-years.

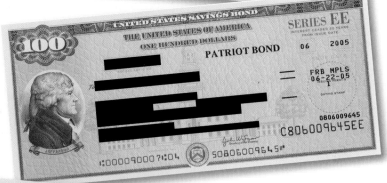

U.S. $200 Series EE Patriot Bond, costs $100 and is guaranteed to double in value over a 20-year period. Can be cashed in after 5 years without penalty and pays interest for up to 30-years. There are also $500, $1000, $5000 and $10,000 denominations available in the Patriot Bond series.

Iraqi Most Wanted playing card reproduction deck. These are the "most wanted" decks, which are most often offered on the Internet, with prices ranging from $2.50 to $20.00. The original "most wanted" decks were issued to troops by the Defense Intelligence Agency and U.S. Central Command in Iraq during April 2003.

Several different sets of Desert Storm trading cards were issued. Here is an example from the Desert Storm Limited Collector's Edition set, card #7, picturing an F-4G Phantom "Wild Weasel" from side and below.

بطل النصر والسلام

One of the Ministry of Culture and information propaganda posters printed at the House of Freedom Press. This one shows Hussein in white dress uniform and identifies him as the "Champion of Victory and Peace".

Another Saddam Hussein poster issued from the Ministry of Culture and Information during his reign in Iraq. This one displays Hussein in military uniform and translates as "The Awesome Pillar, Saddam Hussein, President of the Republic of Iraq and Supreme Commander of the Armed Forces". The printer of this poster is noted at lower left as "House of Freedom Printing".

A more political minded presentation of Hussein from the Ministry of Information, Department of Information, printed at House of Freedom Publishing. Here Hussein wears a traditional Kaffiyeh and ekal head covering and the posters caption translates as "His Excellency, the President, the Leader, Saddam Hussein, May God protect him and watch over him".

صدام حسين حفظه الله ورعاه

دار العربية للطباعة

Again, a smiling Hussein presented by the Ministry of Culture and Information, House of Freedom Press. In dark dress uniform, this time he is identified as "Saddam Hussein, the Most High, the Mighty, the Defiant".

صدام حسين الشموخ، العزة، التحدي

تصوير - حسين محمد علي
طبع دار الحرية للطباعة

وزارة الثقافة والاعلام

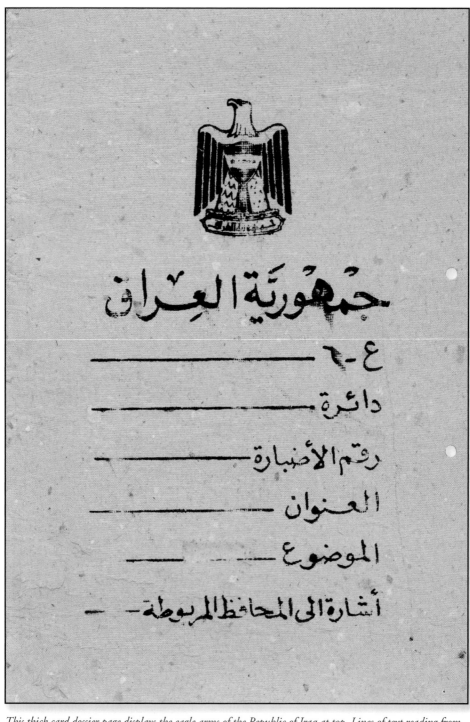

جمهورية العِراق

ع-٦ _____

دائرة _____

رقم الأضبارة _____

العنوان _____

الموضوع _____

أشارة الى المحافظ المربوطة _____

This thick card dossier page displays the eagle arms of the Republic of Iraq at top. Lines of text reading from top to bottom translate as: Republic of Iraq, _____ -6, Department_____, File (or dossier) number_____, Title (or address)_____, Subject_____, Alert (or advice) to the garrison commander. This type of item may have been used to keep records on individuals not thought to be loyal to the regime.

During the first Gulf War, Time magazine really brought the events and effects of the war home to its readers. In February 1991 we saw battles in Khafji, "Stormin' Norman" and the face of real sacrifice.

On the ground and moving into Kuwait, Time captured our troops in action on these covers from February and March issues, 1991.

The U.S. flag is proudly displayed by our troops, on these two Time magazine covers, as they moved into Kuwait City on February 27, 1991.

Stars and Stripes has a long tradition of keeping our troops informed of local news and the news from back home. A real moral booster, it helps those who serve to keep their lives and purpose in focus. This Monday July 4, 2005 Stars and Stripes Mideast edition is printed and delivered by local commands for our soldiers in Afghanistan, Kuwait, Iraq, Bahrain and Qatar.

Security forces kill Saudi Arabia's Al-Qaida head during raid Page 11

STARS AND STRIPES.

Damon Wayans takes the stage for standup Page 19

Petty officer deploys to Afghanistan with Army unit Page 4

Federer dominant in winning third Wimbledon title Back page

Volume 3, No.85 © SS 2005 MIDEAST EDITION

MONDAY, JULY 4, 2005

Free in Deployed Areas

Happy Fourth of July

- Costly gas unlikely to keep Americans at home Page 8
- Washington Monument ready for revelers Page 9

Taking the sting out of live-fire training

Marines share their expertise, make friends in Georgia's army
Pages 6-7

Autographed color photo of King Hussein of Jordan, in military shirt with Kaffiyeh and ekal pinned by gold royal broach. $250.

On a scorching day in 1991, US soldiers in the Desert Storm operation stormed a bunker and captured 6 Iraqi fighters. Spoils of war yield this group of items retrieved from one of those prisoners, including an Iraqi gas mask, a utility pouch, an ammunition harness and a helmet liner. A tag affixed to the harness strap indicates it belonged to "recruit" Hashim Mahan Abdul-Rasul. Value for these artifacts: $150 – $200.

Autographs can be found on cards, in books, on checks or in this case on letters. When the letter contains contents germane to a specific subject the value is generally higher in that field. The Donald Rumsfeld letter illustrated here is on White House letterhead, a plus towards it's value of $75.00. The second letter pictured here, is signed by Robert C. Ode who notes below his name that he is the "oldest of the former hostages in Iran", value $75.

THE WHITE HOUSE
WASHINGTON

February 5, 1975

Dear Mr. Kover:

Thank you for writing. I am pleased to see the thought and effort you are exerting to improve the outlook of our youth and to direct their energies to higher goals.

As you may know, I was a Boy Scout, and in thinking back over my experiences, the attainment of Eagle Scout rank and the ceremony for that occasion when I presented the pin to my Mother was a memorable point for me. It had taken a great deal of effort to reach that achievement, but it had been interesting and worthwhile.

With my best wishes.

Sincerely,

Donald Rumsfeld
Assistant to the President

Mr. Joseph Kover
147 – 40 – 73rd Avenue
Flushing 67, Long Island, New York

Saddam's reward to the surviving family members which made the ultimate sacrifice of a loved one consisted of a small pin back with a large flower arising to the heavens between 2 domes (35mm) and a large brass plaque with the image of a Russian AK-47 rifle, helmet and national flag, referred to as a "Martyr's Plaque" (164mm). A translation of the plaque reads **"And when those who are killed for the cause of God are counted, their Lord restores life upon the gallant dead. To our most noble martyrs. Saddam Hussein"**.

The plaques were manufactured in Italy, but eventually were crafted of a thinner, cheaper metal by the Iraqis. Pin: $9.00 Plaques: Italian brass: $60.00 Baghdad brass-plated tin: $40.00.

Yassir Arafat, chairman of Palestine Liberation Organization (PLO) from 1969 until his death in 2004.
Original hand-signed photos of this very famous leader are hard to come by. This one is a gem and still
accompanied by the original presentation folder. value $400.

Postage stamps are uncommon and quite interesting, including this group of 25 Dinars, ca.1997, with portraits of Saddam Hussein and Salah-al-Din, Kurdish conqueror and ruler in Egypt and Syria in the 12th century. This is yet another example of Saddam placing himself in the company of powerful rulers.

A smiling Saddam Hussein portrait badge, with clear plastic cover and aluminum bronze pin back. In this example Saddam wears a civilian suite and tie. value $5.00.

Another portrait badge shows Saddam in military uniform, legends run across top and bottom. value $5.00.

Shown are examples of both large and small propaganda posters used in Iraq during the hunt for Saddam Hussein. These were posted everywhere there was available space and significant public traffic. Values are about $15.00 for the large poster and $10.00 for the smaller example.

مكافأة

يصل قدرها إلى ٢٥ مليون دولار اميركي

هاتف: ٩٦٤٨١٣٦٦٦٦

البريد الإلكتروني: tips@orha.centcom.mil

مكافأة

أية معلومات تؤدي الى الوقاية من وقوع الاضرار المتعمدة للبنية التحتية العراقية والى منع أعمال العنف ضد قوات التحالف أو تقود الى إعتقال المسؤولين عن هذه الاعمال قد تمنحكم فرصة الحصول على مكافأة مالية تصل قيمتها الى ١١٠ الآف دولار أميركي

الاتصال على الرقم: ٩٦٤ ـ ٨١٣ ـ ٦٦٦٦

البريد الإلكتروني: tips@orha.centcom.mil

Two bumper stickers made for use in promoting the hunt for Saddam, after the Coalition had gained significant control over most major cities in Iraq. Valued at about $6.00 each.

This Iraq-Iran War subscription badge would have been given out to those Iraqi citizens who showed open support, both verbal and economic, for their country during this conflict. value $10.00.

A mid sized poster version of the original 55 most wanted high ranking Ba'ath officials and members of Saddam Hussein's government. The red x's would indicate those individuals who had already been captured, so this poster must have been produced and distributed during the war and occupation period, after invasion, so that service personnel would be familiar with the faces of those individuals whose' capture was still most important to the war effort. This original list of 55 was paired down to make the famous Most Wanted playing card decks. Poster value: $10.00.

Operation Enduring Freedom and Operation Iraqi Freedom are both honored on this large naval patch from 2003. Named on the outer edge are the USS Saipan, USS Ashland, USS Bataan, USS Gunston Hall, USS Kearsarge, USS Ponce, and USS Portland.

A golden eagle graces this HMM 162 velcro backed patch from the Marine Medium Helicopter Squadron 162. This unit is nicknamed the Golden Eagles and serves the purpose of conducting air operations in support of Marine Forces, in addition to working with Naval aviation when needed.

An engraved Fire and Rescue squad plaque from the USS Saipan LHA-2 at Sea Fire Party Flying Squad.

The ever popular engraved Zippo lighter! This one displays the USS Saipan LHA-2 and bears their fire and rescue teams symbol at top.

DC3 WIERZBA

OPERATION IRAQI FREEDOM 2003

U.S.S. SAIPAN LHA - 2

USS IWO JIMA
UNCOMMON VALOR
LHD 7

Another engraved Zippo lighter, this time from the USS Iwo Jima LHD-7.

Three individual stamps, plus a souvenir sheet were issued by Kuwait to commemorate the Iraqi invasion and Desert Storm.

Souvenir sheets are another form of collectible stamps. Kuwait has issued several souvenir sheets with commemorative ties to it's conflicts within the region. This "Thanks to the Coalition" sheet was issued in 1991 at a denomination of 1 Dinar.

Colorful depictions of Invasion day grace these two blocks of four designs each. Denominations on these Kuwait stamps are 50 fils and 150 fils respectively.

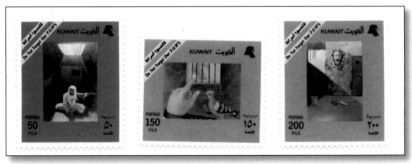

from Kuwait, a somber set of three individual stamps pleads "Do Not Forget Our P.O.W.s".

Interesting agricultural designs highlight this block of four stamps issued for the 12th Gulf Cooperation Council Summit, held in Kuwait in 1991.

A mini sheet of 8 stamps displays the attraction of Expo '92 in Seville, Spain. The designers name and signature are printed at the bottom edge of this sheet issued by Kuwait.

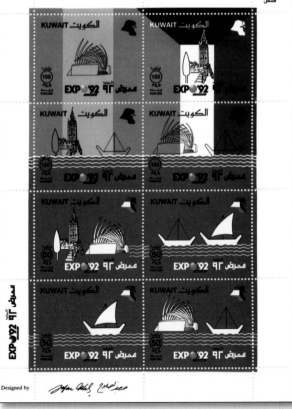

APPENICES

MIDDLE EAST CONFLICTS
A TIMELINE

Lebanese Civil War – 1975-1990

Lebanon's civil war erupted in March 1975, and in 1976 a Syrian-dominated Arab Deterrent Force brought an end to fighting in many areas, however, in 1978 Israel invaded after a Palestinian lead attack. UN Peacekeeping Forces were augmented when Israel installed a Christian-Lebanese militia in border areas. In 1982 Israel invaded again, taking much more land and laying siege to Beirut. Israeli forces started to withdraw in 1985, but it was not until 1990 that those forces were gone. A new Lebanese government was formed on December 24, 1990.

Yemeni War, 1979

Soviet invasion and occupation of Afghanistan, 1979-1988

The Soviet invasion of Afghanistan was a 10-year war fought between the Soviet Red Army against Afghan and foreign fighters. Called the "shooting war" it started in December 1979. Soviet troops eventually withdrew starting in May 1988 and were all out by February 1989.

The war was regarded by many as an unprovoked invasion of one sovereign country by another. In 1983 the United Nations requested that the Soviet Union forces should withdraw from Afghanistan. However, others supported the Soviet Union, regarding the occupation as coming to the rescue of an impoverished ally, or as a pre-emptive war against Islamic terrorists.

Iranian Hostage Crisis, 1979-1981

The hostage crisis was a 444-day event which started when extremists representing the new government of Iran held hostage 66 diplomats and citizens of the United States at the United States embassy compound in Tehran. It began on November 4, 1979 and ended just as Ronald Regan was taking the oath of office as president on January 20, 1981. Incumbent Jimmy Carter did not leave the White House to campaign while the hostages were being held.

Iraq-Iran War, 1980-1988

Iraq invaded Iran in September 1980 in a dispute over the Shatt-al-Arab waterway. The United Nations arranged a cease-fire, which began on August 20, 1988, and in August 1990 Iraq offered peace terms and began the removal of troops from Iranian lands.

Kurdish fight for a homeland, 1980-present

Under the former Iraqi Ba'athist regime, which rulled Iraq from 1968-2003, Kurds were initially granted limited autonomy (1970), and after the Barzani revolt given some high-level political representation in the government. However, for various reasons, including the siding of some Kurds with Iranian forces during the Iran-Iraq war of the 1980s, the regime became opposed to the Kurds and an effective civil war broke out. Iraq was widely condemned for using chemical weapons during this conflict, resulting in the death of thousands of Kurds.

Soldiers from the 34th Infantry Division's 1st Briagade, 168th Infantry Regiment provide security during a mission in Kapisa, Afghanistan. The 168th National Gaurd unit is deployed to Afghanistan in support of Operation Enduring Freedom.

Kurdish regions during the 1990s had *de facto* independence, with fully functioning civil administrations, and were protected by the US-enforced Iraqi no-fly zone, which stopped Iraqi air raids. During this period there were three political/military groups in the area, each claiming the title of Kurdistan's government, which undermined the effectiveness of the Kurdish bid for freedom.

With the fall of the Hussein regime little is known as to how the "Kurdistan" issue will be dealt with in the future. The American-sponsored idea of a Federal Republic, with a relatively high level of autonomy for the Kurds, currently appears to be popular. Steps toward greater autonomy were encouraged when the Iraqi president was elected in 2005.

Israeli invasion of Lebanon, 1982-84

Sudanese Civil War, 1983-2005

The second Sudanese civil war started in 1983, although it is really a continuation of the first civil war of 1955-1972. It took place mostly in southern Sudan, and more than 1.9 million civilians were killed with more than four million forced to flee their homes. The conflict finally ended with the signing of the Naivasha Treaty on January 9, 2005, which grants the south autonomy for six years, to be followed by a referendum on independence.

Israel-Lebanese Border War, 1984-2000

Operation Earnest Will, 1987-88

Called the "Tanker war". Iran attacked Kuwaiti oil tankers in the Gulf. The United States offered protection and engaged in combat with Iran's Navy and Revolutionary Guards.

Arab-Israeli Wars, first Palestinian Intifada, 1987-93

The Intifadas is the uprising by the Palestinians in the territory occupied by Israel since the 1967 war. The Oslo Accords set up a timetable for Palestinian nationhood and the establishment of Palestinian authority.

Afghanistan Civil War, 1988-2001

Somalia Civil War, 1988-2004

The Gulf War, Operations Desert Shield and Desert Storm, 1990-91

The 1991 Gulf war was a conflict between Iraq and a coalition force of 34 nations mandated by the United Nations and under the leadership of the United States. The war began when Iraq invaded Kuwait on August 2, 1990, which was meet with immediate economic sanctions by the United Nations against Iraq. Hostilities commenced in January 1991, resulting in a decisive victory for the coalition forces, which drove Iraqi forces out of Kuwait. The main battles were aerial and ground combat within Iraq, Kuwait and bordering areas of Saudi Arabia. The war did not expand outside the region, although Iraq fired missiles on several Israeli cities.

Iraqi Occupation by United Nation forces, the No-Fly zone, 1992-2003

United States and United Kingdom forces enforced a no-fly zone in the southern portion of Iraq.

Somalia Peacekeeping Mission, 1993-94

Civil War had been a fact of life in Somalia since 1977. In 1991, the northern portion of the country declared its independence as Somaliland; although independent and relatively stable compared to the tumultuous south, it has not been recognized by any foreign government.

Beginning in 1993 a two-year United Nations humanitarian effort (primarily in the south) was able to alleviate famine conditions, but the United National withdrew in Operation United Shield by March 1995 after having suffered many casualties. Order has still not been restored.

Yemeni Civil War, 1994 Pakistani-Sunni-Shiite Conflict, 1995-present

Saudi-Yemen border conflict, 1998

In the summer of 2000, Yemen and Saudi-Arabia signed an international border treaty settling a fifty-year old dispute over the location of the border between the two countries.

Ethiopia-Eritrea War, 1998-2000

The Eritrea-Ethiopian War of May 1998 thru June 2000 between Ethiopia and Eritrea was a continuance of problems relating to the 1993 separation of the two countries. At that time the border was not fully drawn, and several areas were in dispute. Hostilities involving artillery, tanks, ground troops and warplanes led to massive internal displacement in both countries as civilians fled the war zone. Up to a hundred-thousand lives were lost, and the governments of the two countries spent hundreds of millions of dollars in the war effort.

In May 2000, Ethiopia occupied about a quarter of Eritrea's territory, displacing 650,000 people and destroying key components of Eritrea's infrastructure. Having recaptured its territory, Ethiopia declared the war was over. As they were in a strategically vulnerable position, Eritrea was willing to accept a ceasefire, followed by a peace agreement.

War on Terrorism, 2001-present

The War on Terrorism is the term used by the United States government and its allies in the ongoing campaign to destroy individuals and groups determined to be "terrorists" and "terrorist-supporting" states and organizations, with a focus on stopping Islamic terrorism committed by groups such as al-Qaeda.

Following the September 11, 2001 attacks at the World Trade Center and the Pentagon, as well as a high-jacking which was foiled by a crash in Pennsylvania, which in total killed almost 3,000 people, the War on Terrorism became the central focus of United States foreign and domestic policy.

DOD PHOTO BY SPC. JAMES B. SMITH JR., U.S. ARMY

Spc. Jeremy Squirres, with Alpha Company, 101st Military Intelligence Battalion, 3rd Brigade Combat Team, 1st Infantry Division, prepares a Shadow 200 Unmanned Aerial Vehicle for launch at Forward Operating Base Warhorse, Sept. 22, 2004. Alpha Company, 101st MI, operates and maintains the Unmanned Aerial Vehicles for missions in Baqubah, Iraq.

Afghanistan War, 2001-present

The United States invasion of Afghanistan (operation Enduring Freedom) occurred in October 2001, in the wake of the September 11, 2001 attacks on the United States. This marked the beginning of the War on Terrorism response, seeking to out the Taliban and find al-Qaeda mastermind Osama bin Laden. In addition to United States troops, Australia and Canada provided support. The purpose of the invasion was to target al-Qaeda members and to punish the Taliban government in Afghanistan, which has provided support and a haven to Al-Qaeda operatives.

Arab-Israel Wars, second Palestinian Intifada, 2000-05 Sudan-Darfur Conflict, 2003

In early 2003 a rebellion began in Sudan's western providence of Darfur. It was the Arab-dominated Sudanese government against two local rebel groups – the Justice and Equality movement and the Sudanese Liberation Army, during which time the Sudanese government committed terrible atrocities. By the summer of 2004, some 50,000 to 80,000 people had been killed and at least one million had been driven from their homes, causing a major humanitarian crisis in the region.

War in Iraq – Operation Iraqi Freedom and Enduring Freedom, 2003-present.

The 2003 invasion of Iraq was launched by the United States and the United Kingdom on March 20, 2003, with the support from some thirty other governments. The mission's legitimacy has been disputed: the officially stated reason was that Iraq possed "Weapons of Mass Destruction" and the appreciation of the urgency to counter a possible use of those weapons varied greatly among members of the United Nations. After approximately three weeks of fighting, Iraq was occupied by coalition forces and the rule of Saddam Hussein and his Ba'ath Party came to an end. Weapons of mass destruction to be found. Subsequently, the post-invasion period has come to be known as operation "Enduring Freedom." Elections, new monetary policies are under way and soon a new constitution will be adopted.

Sergeant Pete Heap from Charlie Troop, 1-4 Cavalry, 1st Infantry Division finishes searching a minaret in the ruins of Ancient Samarra near Ad Dwr, Iraq during a combat security patrol Nov. 17, 2004 during Operation Iraqi Freedom.

MIDDLE EAST MAP

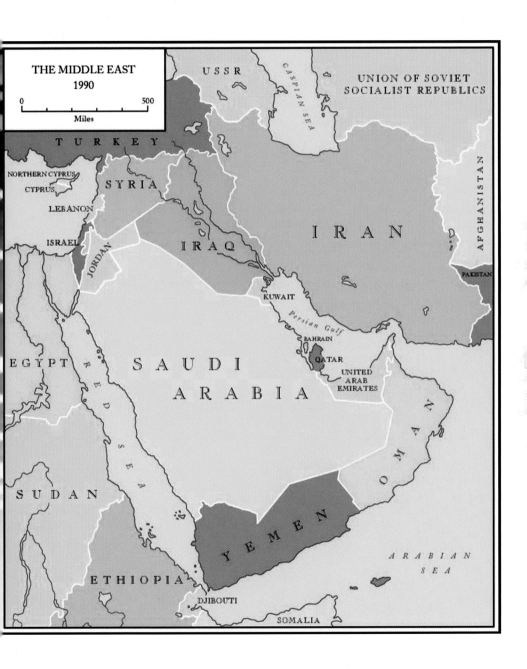

THE MIDDLE EAST
1990

0   500
Miles

USSR

CASPIAN SEA

UNION OF SOVIET
SOCIALIST REPUBLICS

TURKEY

NORTHERN CYPRUS
CYPRUS

SYRIA

LEBANON

ISRAEL

JORDAN

IRAQ

IRAN

AFGHANISTAN

PAKISTAN

KUWAIT

Persian Gulf

BAHRAIN

QATAR

UNITED
ARAB
EMIRATES

EGYPT

RED SEA

SAUDI

ARABIA

OMAN

SUDAN

YEMEN

ARABIAN
SEA

ETHIOPIA

DJIBOUTI

SOMALIA

NUMERALS
AND DATE SYSTEMS

WESTERN	0	½	1	2	3	4	5	6	7	8	9	10	50	100	500	1000
ROMAN			I	II	III	IV	V	VI	VII	VIII	IX	X	L	C	D	M
ARABIC-TURKISH	•	١/٢	١	٢	٣	٤	٥	٦	٧	٨	٩	١٠	٥٠	١٠٠	٥٠٠	١٠٠٠
MAYLAY-PERSIAN	•	١/٢	١	٢	٣	۴	۵	٦ or ۷	٧	٨	٩	١٠	۵٠	١٠٠	۵٠٠	١٠٠٠
EASTERN ARABIC	٥	½	١	٢	٣	٤	٥	٤	٧	٧	٩	١٥	٤١٥	١٥٥	٤١٥٥	١٥٥٥
HYDERABAD ARABIC	٥	١/٢	١	٢	٣	٣	٥	٤	<	٨	٩	١٥	٥٥	١٥٥	٥٥٥	١٥٥٥
EITHIOPIAN	◆		፩	፪	፫	፬	፭	፮	፯	፰	፱	፲	፶	፻	፭፻	፲፻

EITHIOPIAN (tens row): 20 ፳ · 30 ፴ · 40 ፵ · 60 ፷ · 70 ፸ · 80 ፹ · 90 ፺

| HEBREW | | | א | ב | ג | ד | ה | ו | ז | ח | ט | י | נ | ק | תק | תת |

HEBREW (additional row): 20 כ · 30 ל · 40 מ · 60 ס · 70 ע · 80 פ · 90 צ · 200 ר · 300 ש · 400 ת · 600 תר · 700 תש · 800 תת

HEJIRA DATE CONVERSION CHART

JEHIRA DATE CHART

HEJIRA (Hijira, Hegira), the name of the Muslim era (A.H. = Anno Hegirae) dates back to the Christian year 622 when Mohammed "fled" from Mecca, escaping to Medina to avoid persecution from the Koreish tribemen. Based on a lunar year the Muslim year is 11 days shorter.

*=Leap Year (Christian Calendar)

AD	Christian Date	AD	Christian Date	AD	Christian Date
1390	1970, March 9	1411	1990, July 24	1432	2010, December 8
1391	1971, February 27	1412	1991, July 13	1433	2011, November 27*
1392	1972, February 16*	1413	1992, July 2*	1434	2012, November 15
1393	1973, February 4	1414	1993, June 21	1435	2013, November 5
1394	1974, January 25	1415	1994, June 10	1436	2014, October 25
1395	1975, January 14	1416	1995, May 31	1437	2015, October 15*
1396	1976, January 3*	1417	1996, May 19*	1438	2016, October 3
1397	1976, December 23*	1418	1997, May 9	1439	2017, September 22
1398	1977, December 12	1419	1998, April 28	1440	2018, September 12
1399	1978, December 2	1420	1999, April 17	1441	2019, September 11*
1400	1979, November 21	1421	2000, April 6*	1442	2020, August 20
1401	1980, November 9*	1422	2001, March 26	1443	2021, August 10
1402	1981, October 30	1423	2002, March 15	1444	2022, July 30
1403	1982, October 19	1424	2003, March 5	1445	2023, July 19*
1404	1984, October 8	1425	2004, February 22*	1446	2024, July 8
1405	1984, September 27*	1426	2005, February 10	1447	2025, June 27
1406	1985, September 16	1427	2006, January 31	1448	2026, June 17
1407	1986, September 6	1428	2007, January 20	1449	2027, June 6*
1409	1987, August 26	1429	2008, January 10*	1450	2028, May 25
1409	1988, August 14*	1430	2008, December 29		
1410	1989, August 3	1431	2009, December 18		

Afghanistan

Until 1919, coins in Afghanistan were dated by the lunar Islamic Hejira calendar (AH), often with the king's regnal year as a second date. The solar Hejira (SH) calendar was introduced in 1919 (1337 AH, 1298 SH). The rebel Habibullah reinstated lunar Hejira dating (AH 1347-50), but the solar calendar was used thereafter. All coins listed in this volume carry SH dates. The solar Hejira year begins on the first day of spring, about March 21. Adding 621 to the SH year yields the AD year in which it begins.

Ethiopia

Ethiopian coinage is dated by the Ethiopian Era calendar (E.E.), which commenced 7 years and 8 months after the advent of A.D. dating.

Dates on Ethiopian coins can be read as indicated in the following example.

10 + 9 = 90 x 100 = 1900
30 + 6 = 36
1900 + 36 =1936 E.E.

To convert to AD dates add the 7 years and 8 months =1943/4 AD

Iran

COIN DATING

Iranian coins were dated according to the lunar ISLAMIC Hejira calendar until March 21, 1925 (AD), when dating was switched to a new calendar based on the solar Hejira year, indicated by the notation SH. The monarchial calendar system was adopted in 1976 = MS2535 and was abandoned in 1978 = MS2537. The previously used solar Hejira calendar was restored at that time.

AD Date	Isreal/Hebrew	Jewish Era
1970	תש״ל	5730
1971	תשל״א	5731
1972	תשל״ב	5732
1973	תשל״ג	5733
1974	תשל״ד	5734
1975	תשל״ה	5735
1976	תשל״ו	5736
1977	תשל״ז	5737
1978	תשל״ח	5738
1979	תשל״ט	5739
1980	תש״ם	5740
1981	תשמ״א	5741
1981	התשמ״א	5741
1982	התשמ״ב	5742
1983	התשמ״ג	5743
1984	התשמ״ד	5744
1985	התשמ״ה	5745
1986	התשמ״ו	5746
1987	התשמ״ז	5747
1988	התשמ״ח	5748
1989	התשמ״ט	5749
1990	התש״ן	5750
1991	התשנ״א	5751
1992	התשנ״ב	5752
1993	התשנ״ג	5753
1994	התשנ״ד	5754
1995	התשנ״ה	5755
1996	התשנ״ו	5756
1997	התשנ״ז	5757
1998	התשנ״ח	5758
1999	התשנ״ט	5759
2000	התש״ס	5760
2001	התשס״א	5761
2002	התשס״ב	5762
2003	התשס״ג	5763
2004	התשס״ד	5764
2005	התשס״ה	5765

WEB SITES

http://www.armytimes.com/ - a great location for up to date military news

http://www.state.gov/r/pa/ei/bgn/ - Fine for background information on foreign nations

http://www.library.okstate.edu/govdocs/browsetopics/milhist.html - good for links to historical study sites

http://www.uswars.net/links.htm - U.S war history information

http://www.army.mil/cmh-pg/ - U.S. Army Center of Military History

http://www.army.mil/cmh-pg/photos/gulf_war/index.htm - Gulf War photographs

http://www.moapress.com/ - Military medal references

http://www.usmedals.com/store.html?id_medals=0527WB180603 - Military medal retail sales

http://www.militarycoins.com/ - Challenge coin retail sales

http://www.psywarrior.com/links.html - Propaganda leaflet information links

http://www.psywarrior.com/index.html - Propaganda leaflet background information

http://www.psywar.org - Propaganda leaflet information

http://www.susmi.com/ - Military insignia retail sales

http://www.smh-hq.org/ - Society for Military History

http://www.army.mil/A-Z.htm - U.S. Army site

http://carlisle-www.army.mil/usamhi/ - U.S. Army Military history

http://www.asmic.org/nonmemberhome.htm - The American Society of Military Insignia Collectors

http://www.ebay.com/ - Ebay Auctions

U.S. AIR FORCE PHOTO BY STAFF SGT ASHLEY BROKOP

U.S. Army soldiers raise the flag in a ceremony presided by U.S. Amb. John D. Negroponte, signifying the establishment of the new U.S. Embassy Regional Office in Al illa, Iraq, on July 15, 2004.